DATE DUE

			Printed in USA

HIGHSMITH #45230

Women in the Arts

Sarah Bernhardt

He who neglects the arts when he is young
has lost the past and is dead to the future.

—Sophocles, *Fragments*

Sarah Bernhardt

Elizabeth Silverthorne

Introduction by
Congresswoman Betty McCollum
Minnesota, Fourth District
Member, National Council on the Arts

CHELSEA HOUSE
PUBLISHERS
A Haights Cross Communications Company
Philadelphia

CHELSEA HOUSE PUBLISHERS

VP, New Product Development Sally Cheney
Director of Production Kim Shinners
Creative Manager Takeshi Takahashi
Manufacturing Manager Diann Grasse

Staff for SARAH BERNHARDT

Editor Patrick M. N. Stone
Production Assistant Megan Emery
Photo Editor Sarah Bloom
Series & Cover Designer Terry Mallon
Layout 21st Century Publishing and Communications, Inc.

A Haights Cross Communications ◀ Company

www.chelseahouse.com

First Printing

1 3 5 7 9 8 6 4 2

Library of Congress Cataloging-in-Publication Data

Silverthorne, Elizabeth.
   Sarah Bernhardt/by Elizabeth Silverthorne.
      p. cm. — (Women in the arts)
Includes index.
Summary: A biography of the French actress, Sarah Bernhardt.
   ISBN 0-7910-7458-7 (Hardcover)
   1. Bernhardt, Sarah, 1844-1923. 2. Actors—France—Biography.
[1. Bernhardt, Sarah, 1844-1923. 2. Actors and actresses. 3. Women—
Biography.] I. Title. II. Series: Women in the arts (Philadelphia, Pa.)
PN2638.B5S49 2003
792'.028'092—dc21
                                                                2003009498

Table of Contents

Introduction

Congresswoman Betty McCollum
Minnesota, Fourth District
Member, National Council on the Arts

I am honored to introduce WOMEN IN THE ARTS, a continuing series of books about courageous, talented women whose work has changed the way we think about art and society. The women highlighted in this series were persistent, successful, and at times controversial. They were unafraid to ask questions or challenge social norms while pursuing their work. They overcame barriers that included discrimination, prejudice, and poverty. The energy, creativity, and perseverance of these strong women changed our world forever.

Art plays a critical role in all our lives, in every culture, and especially in the education of young people. Art can be serious, beautiful, functional, provocative, spiritual, informative, and illuminating. For all of the women in this series, their respective forms of artistic expression were a creative exploration and their professional calling. Their lives and their work transformed the world's perception of a woman's role in society.

In reading this series, I was struck by common themes evident in these women's lives that can provide valuable lessons for today's young women.

One volume tells the story of Coco Chanel, the first fashion designer to create clothing for women that was both attractive and utile. Chanel was one of the first women to run a large, successful business in the fashion industry. Today, it is hard to imagine the controversy Chanel stirred up simply by making women's clothing beautiful, comfortable, and practical. Chanel understood that women wanted a sense of style and professionalism in their fashion, as men had in theirs.

Chanel's extraordinary success demonstrates that we should not be afraid to be controversial. Even today, women of all ages worry far too much about stepping on toes or questioning authority. To make change, in our own lives or in our community, we need to stand up and speak out for our beliefs. The women of this series often defied convention and ruffled some feathers, but they never stopped. Nina Simone sang beautifully, but she also spoke out against the injustice of racism, regardless of how it affected her career.

It is equally important for us women to ask ourselves, "What do I want from my life?" We all struggle to answer this deceptively simple question. It takes courage to answer it honestly, but it takes far more courage to answer the question and then *act* on that answer. For example, Agnes de Mille realized she had "nothing to lose by being direct." She stuck to her vision for *Rodeo,* insisted on the set and composer she envisioned, and eventually produced her ballet—the way she wanted to. She believed in her vision, and the result was a great success. Dorothea Lange, having decided she wanted to become a photographer, asked for photography jobs, even though she had no experience and it was a profession that few women pursued.

In our society, we expect that all people should be treated with respect and dignity, but this has not always been true. Nina Simone faced discrimination and overcame social norms that promoted racial injustice. She confronted prejudice and disrespect directly, sometimes refusing to perform when an audience was unruly or rude. One evening, when she was only eleven years old, she even delayed her performance until her own parents were allowed to sit in the front row—seats that they had been asked to vacate for white people. Her demand for respect took courage.

Women's equality not only benefits women, but also brings a unique perspective to the world. For example, the brilliance of Dorothea Lange's photography was in large part due to her empathy for her subjects. She knew that to tell their story, she needed to earn their trust and to truly understand their lives.

Each of these women used her art to promote social justice. Coco Chanel used her designs to make women's lives easier and more comfortable, while Nina Simone was as committed to civil rights as she was to her music. Dorothea Lange's photographs convinced Washington of the need to establish sanitary camps for migrant families, and Virginia Woolf's writing pushed the question of equal rights for women.

Because the women in these books, and so many others like them, took risks and challenged society, women today have more opportunity than ever before. We have access to equal education, and we are making great strides in the workplace and in government.

As only the second woman from Minnesota ever elected to serve in Congress, I know how important it is to have strong female role models. My grandmothers were born in a time when women did not have the right to vote, but their granddaughter is now a Member of Congress. Their strength, wisdom, and courage inspire me. Other great women, such as Congresswoman Barbara Jordan and Congresswoman Shirley Chisholm, also inspired me with their leadership and determination to overcome gender and racial discrimination to serve in Congress with distinction.

Dorothea Lange once said, "I have learned from everything, and I'm constantly learning." I know that I too am constantly learning. I hope the women in this series will inspire you to learn and to lead with courage and determination. Art, as a profession or a hobby, can be either an expression or an agent of change. We need to continue to encourage women to add their voices to our society through art.

The women profiled in this series broke barriers, followed their hearts, refused to be intimidated, and changed our world. Their lives and successes should be a lesson to women everywhere. In addition, and importantly, they created lasting and meaningful art. I hope that you will enjoy this series as much as I have.

"The Bernhardt"

I have, thanks to my travels, added to my stock all the superstitions of other countries. I know them all now, and in any critical moment of my life, they all rise up in armed legions for or against me.

—Sarah Bernhardt, quoted in *The Memoirs of Sarah Bernhardt*

COMING HOME

Sarah Bernhardt stood beside the captain on the bridge of the ship *America*, peering through the haze, straining for a glimpse of the French shoreline. As usual, she wore a long white dress and was completely enveloped in furs, veils, and scarves. It was May 15, 1881, and she and her acting troupe were returning from a triumphant seven-month American tour, having visited fifty cities and given 156 performances.

A steamer loaded with reporters, friends, and family of the returning travelers was bearing down on the *America*. At

The Divine Sarah Bernhardt. Bernhardt is considered one of the greatest actresses of all time; the public's adulation for her was rivaled only by its frequent sense of scandal over her behavior and lifestyle. In a seemingly endless performance of heartfelt expression, she lived as though her life and art were one, and she became legendary in her own time. This luminous image of her was painted by the graphic artist Paul Berthon (1872–1909), a leader of the Art Nouveau movement, around 1901.

this moment, however, there was only one person she wanted to see. Searching the deck of the approaching steamer with her binoculars, she found the one she was looking for—her son, 16-year-old Maurice. Crying out in joy, she clung to the railing and turned so white that her alarmed companions quickly administered smelling salts. As Maurice reached the top of the boarding ladder, she threw herself into his arms. It was a touching, dramatic scene, and a perfect illustration of the difficulty Bernhardt found in separating her life and her art, even when her feelings were most genuine.

Seeing that the harbor was filled with more than a hundred rowboats and small sailboats, all decorated with flags and banners, Bernhardt asked a reporter if it was a holiday. Yes, he told her, a holiday in her honor. Pointing to the hundreds of people lining the wharf, he informed her that packed trains had brought her fans from Paris to Le Havre to greet her return. As she disembarked from the ship onto a red carpet, an invisible orchestra played, sailors offered flowers, and a welcoming committee waited under a red velvet marquee. Afterward, she was told that she made an eloquent reply to the welcome speeches, but she could not remember making one: "My heart had not stopped beating with excitement and joy. My mind was full of a thousand things accumulated over seven months. . . ." (*My Double Life*, 308)

LASTING IMPRESSIONS

Back in America, "the Bernhardt" (as reporters liked to refer to her) had left a lasting impression. Stories of her mesmerizing acting, her enchanting voice, her vibrant personality, and her eccentric personal habits would not fade from the daily papers for weeks.

The huge success of the tour was due to the efforts of Edward Jarrett, surely one of the best public-relations managers of all time. His ability to titillate the general public with advance publicity and to make profitable arrangements for his clients with theater managers was legendary in France, England, and the United States. It was he who had suggested the tour to Bernhardt, teasing her imagination with images of golden coins.

During the tour, fascinated American theatergoers, as well as thousands who had never been in a theater at all, devoured the stories that appeared daily in their papers and journals. They scrutinized the lifestyle of this phenomenal French-woman, her appearance, her every word and gesture.

Every detail was discussed of "the Bernhardt Special," too, the grand private train in which Bernhardt traveled across the country. Bernhardt, of course, occupied the Palace Car, with its inlaid wood, stained glass, Turkish carpets, sofas, zebra skins, and piano. She also had a private dining room with a table for ten, complete with linens, china, crystal, and two chefs. Her bedroom on the train contained a brass bed, a mahogany dressing table, and a gilded pier glass. At the end of the car was an observation platform with comfortable chairs where Bernhardt could sit and watch the passing scenery, satisfying her curiosity about the endlessly intriguing United States. Three Pullman cars for the rest of the company completed the train. The troupe's costumes, heavy luggage, and scenery went ahead on a special freight train, and for both trains all tracks were cleared of other traffic.

Every bit of gossip, no matter how blatantly exaggerated, was hashed and rehashed in drawing rooms and farmhouse kitchens across America. Was her leading man, the actor Angelo, also her lover? Did she really eat only mussels all day? Did she sleep in a coffin? Did she buy a pet alligator in Louisiana and name it Ali-Gaga, and did the alligator eat her little dog? Did she sleep with a pearl-handled pistol under her five satin pillows? Had she torn a fin from an enormous whale to use in her corset?

Denunciations from the pulpit by bishops and other members of the clergy—unsolicited publicity—also whetted the public's appetite for more information about "the Bernhardt." These religious leaders warned of contact with this harlot who had an illegitimate son. They considered her a seductress who had come to America to corrupt its

Perhaps the original diva, Sarah Bernhardt rarely lost an opportunity to capitalize on her immense talent—or on her international reputation. In fact, she eventually became almost as famous for her numerous farewell performances as for her acting. Cornelia Otis Skinner, one of Bernhardt's principal biographers, cites a bit of doggerel entitled "Boo-Hoo" that appeared in *The New York Globe* in 1912 in celebration of one of Bernhardt's many long good-byes:

> Who's done Camille in ev'ry clime
>> From here to Zanzibar,
> And trickled briny tears enough
>> To float a man-o'-war?
> Who did it when our grandma was
>> A lassie blithe and gay?
> Who'll still be doing it no doubt
>> When Baby Doll is gray?
> Who needs but pack her gladsome rags
>> And hit the farewell trail
> Whene'er the treasurer reports
>> She's running out of kale?
> Who slips it o'er in perfect French,
>> Assures US that it's art,
> And hauls our Yankee shekels
>> From the show-shop in a cart?
> Who makes us say "How wonderful!"
>> And "Mabel, ain't it fine!"
> And wonder what it's all about?
>> Why Bernhardt the Divine!

(Skinner, 167)

citizens by performing immoral plays. These warnings only succeeded in attracting Americans, who flocked to the theaters, causing every performance to sell out. Many who attended out of morbid curiosity left the theater dazzled and enchanted by a spellbinding performance.

At times, her enormous popularity was almost her undoing. In more than one city, mobs of hysterical greeters managed to separate her from her protective escorts. Jarrett once rescued her from an adoring crowd by leading her down a fire escape. Americans had adopted the craze of "*le autograph*," and they thrust programs and scraps of paper at her to sign at every opportunity. Some even asked her to sign the cuffs of their shirts or other parts of their clothing. When one young woman couldn't make her pen work, she frantically bit her arm to draw blood for ink. Another, in trying to cut a snippet of Bernhardt's hair, missed her target and cut an expensive ostrich feather from the star's hat.

THE INDOMITABLE BERNHARDT

The French troupe performed *La Dame aux Camélias* (*The Lady of the Camellias*) 75 times in America. Of the eight different plays in the company's repertoire, it was far and away the favorite. But to Bernhardt's puzzlement, the Americans insisted on calling it *Camille* and seemed to think that was the name of the main character. In fact, there is no one named Camille in the play. The main character is Marguérite Gauthier, a repentant sinner, a role Bernhardt played with such deeply touching compassion that audiences sobbed during her death scene and left the theater emotionally drained.

After giving 27 performances in New York, the troupe began its arduous journey across the country. In addition to numerous performances in the larger cities—Boston, Montreal, Philadelphia, Chicago, St. Louis, Baltimore, and others—there were many one-night engagements in

The Bernhardt arrives. Adopting the motto "*Quand même*"—roughly, "in spite of it all"—Bernhardt applied her indefatigable will and character to the challenges of life, continually rising to brilliant success. Her grace, natural charm, and luminous presence, both on the stage and off, commanded an even deeper respect given her fear of her own audiences: The "beloved monster" often paralyzed her with *le trac*, or stage fright.

smaller towns. The tour proved to be a severe test even for the indefatigable Bernhardt, who had a miraculous ability to rejuvenate herself after strenuous ordeals. She could lie down on a bed or on the carpet, announce that she would sleep for 20 or 40 minutes, and awaken at the appointed time thoroughly refreshed. Her health had been frail and troubling to her family and friends since her childhood, and she had a tendency to faint when overcome, physically or emotionally, by things beyond her control.

Her greatest assets in facing the challenges of life were her courage and indomitable will. Before she was grown, she adopted the motto that would become her rally cry for years to come. It was "*Quand même*," meaning roughly "nevertheless" or "in spite of it all." Eventually she would have this motto embroidered on her napkins, pillowcases, and bedspreads. It appeared in gold on the flag that flew over her retreat on Belle Île. When she suffered the paralyzing stage fright that attacked her periodically, she would scrawl this in lipstick on her dressing room mirror before she went to face the audience, the "beloved monster" awaiting her.

She used the motto defiantly when someone opposed her plans to take a risk, whether it be with her physical safety or with her career. As she grew older, she used it to defy the onset of old age. The most famous example is when at the age of 65 she played the role of 19-year-old Joan of Arc. When asked her age in the play, Bernhardt-as-Joan turned to face the audience and replied in her crystal-clear voice, "*Dix-neuf ans*" — "Nineteen years." This never failed to elicit thunderous applause; to the audience, she *was* the teenaged martyr.

Throughout her life, Bernhardt suffered severe injuries to her leg in falls. In 1893, for example, when she was playing Tosca in *La Tosca*, someone misplaced a thick mattress for her stage fall. She leaped off the parapet of the castle onto the bare stage and suffered a severe injury. Despite pain, she continued her tours and performances until gangrene set in and, in 1915, the leg had to be amputated.

For the last eight years of her life, Bernhardt maintained a rigorous schedule, performing roles in which she could be carried on and off stage in a litter, adorned in rich clothing and jewelry like an empress. During World War I, she traveled to the front to make patriotic speeches and perform skits for the soldiers. In 1916, she began a final tour of America, and in 1921 she played her final season on the London stage. She continued to perform new roles in Paris, though, and in 1923, the year of her death, she helped to film a movie for a Hollywood company.

"Energy creates energy," Bernhardt liked to say. "It is by spending oneself that one becomes rich." And few people have ever spent themselves more freely than this tiny French actress. She worked incredibly hard at her profession. After giving matinee and evening performances, she might study for a new role until three or four o'clock in the morning. She brought new life to the stage in her interpretations of classic roles like Phaedra (in Jean Racine's *Phèdre*) and created new characters in contemporary drama such as Victorien Sardou's *Tosca*. Her interpretation of the heroine in *La Dame aux Camélias* became the standard for all other actresses to follow. Her long, brilliant career, which had begun in France's two national theaters, continued in England and America and expanded through several rigorous world tours.

Her boundless energy invigorated not only her career, but also her life. "If there's anything more remarkable than watching Sarah act," declared Sardou, "it's watching her live." (Skinner, xvii) She was eager to see and to try anything that interested her—and almost everything did. In addition to acting, she managed a theater. She took up painting, sculpting, writing, fishing, and hunting alligators. She collected wild animals as pets, explored a coal mine, fired a cannon at a firearms factory, flew in a hot-air balloon, and,

La Dame aux Camélias poster by Alphonse Mucha. In what would become perhaps her best-known role, Sarah Bernhardt played the part of Marguérite Gauthier in *La Dame aux Camélias* [*The Lady of Camellias*]. The intensity of the role—Marguérite's illness, her redemption through love, her selfless sacrifice, and her tragic reunion—suited Bernhardt's intensity perfectly. Her passionate performance in the role attracted such attention that the show was performed 75 times in a single American tour. Mucha ranks with Paul Berthon at the forefront of Art Nouveau; beginning in 1894 with Bernhardt's *Gismonda* at the Renaissance Theater, Mucha formed a long and profitable relationship with Bernhardt. He painted dozens of publicity images of her, many of which were used to sell products such as cigars and cookies.

despite her adamant opposition to capital punishment, attended four executions. To her, nothing seemed impossible. When she was given a lifesaver's medal after a benefit performance for boatmen, she responded in her usual impetuous way. Throwing out her arms as if to embrace the audience, she cried out, "I shall save someone! I promise to save someone! It's true I can't swim, but it doesn't matter! I shall learn!" (Gold, 189) No doubt, at that moment she believed she would—*quand même.*

As the horizons of Bernhardt's life expanded, the entire world became her stage, and she played her role as its main character. After she became an international celebrity, she often said, "I am the most lied-about woman in the world!" This may have been true, but, as she well knew, it was often her outrageous behavior and her own scandalous remarks that added to the stories circulated about her. For over 50 years, Sarah Bernhardt was the most famous and notorious

THE MEDIA REMEMBER SARAH BERNHARDT

Sarah Bernhardt is dead at age 78. Last night, the famous actress passed away peacefully. At her bedside, four doctors were struggling against hope to retain the spark of life, so that she might be able to complete the cinema film which was intended to be the precursor of her "final farewell tour." Only Sarah Bernhardt's tremendous vitality explains her long battle against death. Kidney disease, which began ten years ago, threatened her life two years later. Yesterday morning she turned to one of her doctors and said: "Even if I leave, I have done my duty, and the world will not forget."

—*The International Herald Tribune,* March 27, 1923

actress in the world. She loved to shock and amaze people, and when she wrote her memoir, she called it *My Double Life*—an appropriate title for the biography of one who could not separate her life and her art.

2

Childhood

1844–1860

He who is incapable of feeling strong passions, of being shaken by anger, of living in every sense of the word, will never be a good actor. . . .

—Sarah Bernhardt, *The Art of the Theatre* (1924)

MILK BLOSSOM

In writing her memoirs, Bernhardt did not bother to clear up speculations and rumors regarding her parents and their origins. Her Jewish mother, Judith, might have come from Germany or Holland. Her father might have been Paul Morel, a French naval officer, as listed in some official documents. Or, perhaps he was Edouard Bernhardt, a brilliant young French lawyer whose name her mother adopted. Bernhardt referred to her father only as "father."

When Sarah was born on October 23, 1844, Judith was only

Sarah Bernhardt by Giuseppe de Nittis. **The hardships of Bernhardt's childhood, especially her limited connection with her mother in the early years, may have contributed to the depth of dramatic emotion that she was able to express throughout her life and career. This portrait by the Neapolitan artist Giuseppe de Nittis, who is known primarily for his skill at etching, was painted before 1884.**

16 years old. A beautiful girl with a lovely face and figure, Judith had been a milliner before arriving in France to seek her fortune. Perhaps she could have become a governess or a seamstress, but she thought either option was too dull and poorly paid. In the 1840s, among the aristocracy and nobility of Paris, a clever, attractive young woman could set herself up as a courtesan if

she could attract wealthy patrons to support her lifestyle. It was almost a respectable profession; many people admired these women who knew how to entertain lavishly, dress elegantly with style and grace, appreciate art and the theater, and please the men who sponsored them. It was a precarious position and one that required constant close attention. Being able to travel about Europe with one's current lover was also necessary. A demanding baby was not an asset.

Judith's solution was to send Sarah to live with a wet nurse in Brittany, a considerable distance from Paris. The nurse called her Milk Blossom, the only name Sarah knew during her early years. The woman was a good-hearted, illiterate farm peasant, who cared for the child as well as she knew how. One day, when the nurse had been called to work in the fields, she left the baby Milk Blossom in a highchair under the care of her invalid husband. Sarah soon managed to work her way out of her highchair and rolled onto the edge of the blazing fireplace, where her clothing caught fire.

Alerted by the bedridden husband's screams, neighbors rushed in and dumped the smoking baby in a pail of fresh milk. Then all the neighbors brought butter to make poultices to put on the delicate burned skin. Sarah's aunts were notified and managed to reach her mother, who was traveling in Belgium with Baron Larrey, who served as physician to Emperor Napoleon III. Soon a succession of elegant carriages arrived in front of the humble cottage. Sarah's account of the incident reveals her understanding of the nature of this mother from whom she could never win the unconditional love she craved:

> Mama, ravishingly beautiful . . . gave money to everybody. She would have given her golden hair, her childlike feet, and her very life to save this child about whom she had been so little concerned only a week before. Yet she was just as sincere in her despair and her love as she had been in her unconscious forgetfulness. (*My Double Life*, 4)

For six weeks, Judith, her sister Rosine (an even more notorious courtesan than Judith), and a young doctor stayed while Sarah recuperated from the accident. Then Judith moved Sarah, along with the nurse and her husband, to a cottage in Paris on the banks of the River Seine and resumed her travels. She asked Sarah's aunts to look in on the child, but they were too busy to take the time. Judith herself sent money, candy, and toys. For the next few years, the rough peasants were the only family Sarah knew. When the nurse's husband died, she married a concierge. Not knowing how to write and not having an address for Judith, the nurse moved her five-year-old charge to a new home without informing anyone.

The new home was situated at the entrance of a large estate. After living near the sea and a river, the huge gray stones of the gateway and lack of windows in the house depressed the sensitive child, who found the setting dark and ugly. Sarah lost her appetite and grew pale and anemic. Through a strange coincidence, she was rescued from this dismal life in what she later deemed a miracle.

One day as she was playing in the courtyard, she heard a familiar voice and looked up to see the concierge showing two elegant ladies about the estate grounds. Her thin little body began to shake as she recognized her aunt Rosine. Throwing herself at her aunt, she buried her face in her furs, laughing, sobbing hysterically, and ripping her lace sleeves. Amazed at finding her niece in this place, Aunt Rosine stroked her hair and tried to calm her. Then she emptied the contents of her purse into the hands of the nurse and promised to come back for Sarah the next day.

But Sarah had learned not to trust the promises of adults in her life, and she did not believe this playful, charming, self-centered aunt. As the good nurse held the distraught child to a window to watch her aunt's departure, the nurse tried to convince Sarah that her aunt would return. In a fit of despair

Sarah hurled herself from the nurse's arms onto the pavement at her aunt's feet. She awoke in a large, sweet-smelling bed in a bedroom with large windows. She had broken her arm and her kneecap, but she had escaped her dreary surroundings. Her mother returned once again from her travels to care for her daughter. It took two years for the fragile child to recover from the terrible fall and her run-down condition. During that time, she was happy to receive all the cuddling and love that was offered her in her aunt's and her mother's lively households.

BOARDING SCHOOL

At eight years old, Sarah was unable to read, write, or count. Obviously, she needed schooling, and as Judith found herself pregnant again, it seemed most convenient to send Sarah away to boarding school. She chose Madame Fressard's school for young ladies.

Escorted by her mother, Aunt Rosine, and three of their admirers, Sarah was given into Madame Fressard's care along with instructions from Judith. Her unruly hair was to be brushed a hundred strokes before it was combed. For tea, she was to be fed on alternate days the fancy preserves and chocolates brought with her. And finally, Judith handed Madame Fressard a large jar of cold cream of her own making which was to be rubbed on Sarah's face, neck and hands nightly. Judith announced grandly that she would pay double for the laundry, but, as Sarah recalled, her sheets like everyone else's were changed once a month. Her troop of escorts departed to enjoy dinner at a fashionable cabaret, and Sarah was left to be "dragged off to the cage in which I was to be imprisoned."(*My Double Life*, 9)

The two years she spent at the school turned out to be relatively happy ones. She liked the motherly Madame Fressard, and for the first time in her life, she was with girls her own age. She learned to read, write, count, and sing round

Female students attend a cookery class in a French school. At eight years of age, Bernhardt entered boarding school for the first time, and she would spend the rest of her childhood in a succession of structured environments for young ladies. These experiences provided opportunities for Sarah to learn skills essential to the art of acting and to associate with girls of her own age.

songs like "Frère Jacques." She learned manners and how to embroider handkerchiefs. She especially liked the walks they took on Thursdays and Sundays because of the sense of freedom they gave her.

Visits to the large estate of her aunt and uncle Faure provided another escape from the routine of school. Sarah was not fond of her prim and proper aunt Henriette, who called her a gypsy and constantly criticized her. But she adored her gentle uncle Faure, and enjoyed playing with her two cousins. The three of them spent hours fishing in the little brook that ran across the estate.

Despite the orderly discipline of life at the school, Sarah was subject to violent fits of temper, which resulted in severe bouts of illness. When these bouts happened, she was sent to the infirmary to recover alone. For less traumatic offenses, there were Miss Caroline and her ruler. Never in her life did Sarah accept criticism with resignation. When the girls made fun of her appearance, laughing at her kinky hair or thin body, she flew at them, kicking and screaming with rage. Then Miss Caroline would appear, and the combatants were required to hold out their arms with fingers folded tightly over thumbs. Smack! Smack! Smack! The wide ebony ruler would descend on tender knuckles, bringing tears to eyes. Many years later as an adult, when she again saw Miss Caroline, Sarah instinctively hid her hands behind her back.

Judith came to visit Sarah twice during the two years she was at the school. On one occasion, she came to see the children perform a little play. Sarah had the role of Queen of the Fairies. When she peeked through the curtain and saw that no members of her family were present, she went on to perform the first scenes with confidence. But when she suddenly saw her mother and Aunt Rosine and two escorts entering the door at the back of the hall, she began shaking and every line fled from her head. She fled sobbing from the stage in her first agonizing attack of stage fright—an emotional torture that would plague her even after she came to be considered the greatest actress in the world.

Having adjusted to the school routine, Sarah assumed that she would remain at Madame Fressard's for several more years. Therefore, she was shocked when one day, without warning, her aunt Rosine appeared to withdraw her from the school. Her parents had decided she should enter a convent school to further her education.

The idea of having her fate decided so arbitrarily threw Sarah into a rage. She shrieked and rolled on the floor, hurling reproaches at her mother and aunts and at Madame Fressard for not finding a way to keep her at the school. For two hours she struggled, escaping into the garden, climbing a tree, and throwing herself into a muddy pool before she was finally subdued, dressed, and carried off in her aunt's carriage.

When she arrived at her aunt's home, she had a high fever. After she recovered her equilibrium, she was sent to her aunt Henriette Faure's for three weeks while the family awaited Judith's return from abroad. In the meantime, her cousin helped mark Sarah's uniforms and personal belongings with the initials "SB" in red thread. Her uncle gave her a silver place setting and goblet, and her aunt gave her a little scapular that had been blessed. When Judith arrived, her aunt and uncle prepared a farewell dinner. Sarah enjoyed being the center of attention, although she was unsure she would enjoy the convent.

In *My Double Life* (14), Bernhardt says that her father told her if she behaved well at the convent, he would return in four years to get her, and they would take some fine trips together. "I'll be as good as Aunt Henriette," she promised, making everybody laugh. That visit, she said, was the last time she saw her father, who died abroad when she was 12 or 13.

CONVENT LIFE

Notre Dame du Grandchamp, an Augustine convent school near Versailles, was originally founded as a school for daughters of the nobility in 1768. It still took some influence to be admitted, and one of Judith's patrons, the Duc de Morny (half brother of Louis-Napoleon), furnished that influence. The school's prospectus promised, in addition to inspiring its students to piety, "to develop their intelligence and good judgment; to embellish their minds with all useful knowledge; to contribute, as much as possible, toward making their company agreeable and their virtues sweet."(Gold, 20)

That Sarah did not quite meet all of these goals was not for want of effort by the nuns in charge of the school. She was not quite nine when she entered the school in autumn of 1853. The mother superior, Mère Sainte-Sophie, who was kind and merry, quickly won Sarah's heart and became her beloved mentor. The mother superior worked patiently to guide the willful child, who sometimes used language that shocked the nuns and slapped one sister who attempted to force a comb through her tangled hair.

Sarah did well in studies that interested her. She hated spelling and arithmetic and disliked piano lessons. In drawing class, though, she showed a gift that she was to develop later in life. Geography fascinated her, making her dream of far away lands. Deportment lessons made her giggle, but nevertheless, she was learning behavior, such as how to cross a room gracefully, curtsy, remove a glove, and carry a handkerchief— all skills basic to the art of acting.

Having her own garden plot was one of her great pleasures at school. She loved the flowers the gardener helped her to grow and the insects she kept in cages. Few of the other girls accepted her invitations to view her pet crickets, grass snakes, lizards, and spiders. She probably had little help in catching the flies with which she fattened her spiders.

Sarah rarely saw her family during her six years at Grand-champ. She spent brief vacations with Aunt Henriette and only occasionally with her mother. Another baby, Régina, had joined the household. Judith said that Régina, like Sarah's sister Jeanne, had arrived in a tulip. No one seemed concerned that neither child had a father to claim as her own. What bothered Sarah was that her mother was openly and almost exclusively devoted to the beautiful Jeanne. The needs of her oldest daughter seemed to concern Judith less than ever.

It's small wonder that the abandoned child became increasingly influenced by the Christian faith with which she was surrounded. She loved the beauty of the rituals, the candles, the

Bernhardt during her 1891 world tour. Bernhardt's repeated bouts with illness and "fits" resulted in extreme emotional and physical exhaustion and led her doctors to believe that she would die at an early age. This inspired what is described as an "obsession with death" in Bernhardt as a young girl. It was during this period that she acquired her famous coffin, which intensified her mystique—and fed the public's sense of her as otherworldly—over the years.

incense, the chanting, and the mystery of the Mass. The Virgin Mary was her ideal, and Mother Sainte-Sophie her earthly model. She felt mystic yearnings and imagined herself dying at the foot of the altar lying under a black cloak emblazoned with a glowing white cross. She felt happy thinking of the horrified reactions of the nuns and students to such a scene.

When Sarah was 13, it was announced that the archbishop of Paris was coming to visit the convent. The buildings and the grounds were scoured and polished from top to bottom. Speeches and music were prepared, and a play was written in his honor. Sarah was distressed not to be given a part in the play. Her best friend, Louise, received the coveted role of the angel Raphael, and Sarah became her coach, memorizing every word of the part. When the timid Louise collapsed from stage fright during dress rehearsal, Sarah leaped to the platform and volunteered to take the part. Her offer was accepted, and she performed her stage debut for the archbishop of Paris in a long, white robe with paper wings and halo.

Her performance was a great success, and the archbishop promised to return for her baptism in the spring. Before that happened, he was killed, and for days Sarah was devastated. The baptism took place in the spring with another cleric presiding. Judith and Aunt Rosine came to the ceremony, bringing Sarah's half sisters, Jeanne and Régina, so they also could be baptized. In place of fathers, Judith brought three fashionable clubmen to serve as sponsors.

Following her First Communion, Sarah became even more of a religious fanatic. Her occasional violent tantrums were followed by equally impressive demonstrations of repentance. One frosty night, she slipped from her bed, telling her room-mates she was going to take a nosegay to the Blessed Mother and have a talk with the angel Raphael. Barefoot and dressed only in her nightgown, she made her way to the chapel. At daybreak, the sisters found her half frozen in a state of ecstasy and on the verge of pneumonia.

When she had recovered enough to travel, her mother and Aunt Henriette took her to a mountain resort in the Pyrenees, in southeastern France on the border with Spain. After recovering her health, she returned to Grandchamp for a few more terms. At the age of 15, against her wishes, she was withdrawn from Grandchamp and taken to live in her mother's house.

FAMILY LIFE

A certain Mademoiselle Brabender was employed to come to the house daily as a tutor for Sarah and her sisters. Although Sarah became fond of Mademoiselle Brabender and tried to please her, she longed to return to the convent school. Régina was a noisy, demanding child, and Sarah was so jealous of her sister Jeanne, she could take no pleasure in her company. She despised her mother's entertainment and if pressed to join them would go into a fainting act or spill something over her dress to spoil it.

The person for whom Sarah felt the most affection was Madame Guérard, a widow who lived in the apartment over her mother's. With her, Sarah found total acceptance and a devotion that nourished her spirit. This warm, loving person would become her best friend and eventually her lady-in-waiting, social secretary, traveling companion, and anything else Sarah needed her to be. The restless, lonely teenager spent her happiest hours in the company of this gentle friend.

Toward the end of her life, Bernhardt told a grandchild, "Our family, which is decided for us, scarcely matters. Only the people we love count, and above all, the family we create for ourselves." (*Sarah Bernhardt, My Grandmother*, 21)

Because she was sickly, extremely thin with a persistent cough, and occasionally spit up blood, doctors whom Judith called to examine Sarah predicted she would die early as a result of consumption, or tuberculosis. Consequently, death became an obsession with the young girl, who visited the Paris morgue to view the bodies on display. In her memoirs, Bernhardt says that it was at about this time that she acquired her much-publicized coffin.

Feeling herself doomed to an early death, she begged her mother to buy her a pretty coffin. Judith at first refused, but at Sarah's insistence, her mother finally purchased a rosewood coffin lined with white satin for her. While still in her teens, Sarah had her picture taken lying in the coffin. Later, a professional photographer made a more sophisticated photograph showing Sarah lying with hands crossed over her chest with candles, flowers, and palm branches added to the scene. This picture was widely disseminated, and the coffin became part of her legend.

While she still lived, decisions about her future had to be made. At 15, she had reached the legal age for marriage in France, and there were men in her mother's circle who would consent to marry her. Or, like her mother and Aunt Rosine, she could become a courtesan if she could learn to control her temper and display more willingness to please. Or, she could become a nun, as she often expressed a desire to be.

One afternoon, Sarah was told to appear in her mother's salon for a conference that would decide her future. After some discussion, the adults at the council agreed that the only sensible plan was for Sarah to marry. Lifting her face toward heaven, she declared she would marry only God; she had decided to become a nun. The Duc de Morny, who had connections with the theater, patted Sarah's cheek and, calling her a born actress, said, "send her to the Conservatoire." (Gold, 30–31)

Dismayed, Sarah, who had an unfavorable impression of the lives of actresses, fled the room. That evening she was taken to the Comédie Française to see her first real play, and her opinion underwent a dramatic change. "When the curtain slowly rose I thought I was going to faint," she wrote in her memoirs. "It was, in fact, the curtain of my life which was rising." (*My Double Life*, 35)

Learning to Act

1860–1870

To be a good actor . . . it is necessary to have a firmly tempered soul, to be surprised at nothing, to resume each minute the laborious task that has barely just been finished.

—Sarah Bernhardt, *The Art of the Theatre* (1924)

STUDYING AT THE CONSERVATOIRE

Dating to the reign of Louis XVI, the Conservatory of Music and Drama was considered the finest drama school in the world. To enter the Conservatoire, applicants were required to audition before an admissions committee. Although Bernhardt had the advantage of being sponsored by her mother's powerful friends (including the Duc de Morny and the elder Alexandre Dumas), she had to qualify by winning the approval of the formidable committee members.

She studied diction with an instructor whose pedantic

The Conservatoire National Supérieur de Musique. At the age of 15, a young girl needed to consider the options for her future. At the time, marriage, the convent, and the life of a courtesan were among the more commonly recognized paths; Bernhardt's mother had followed the last of the three. Hearing the news that she was to marry, Sarah launched into a reaction so dramatic and so compelling that her talent for the stage was recognized immediately. It was decided that she should attend the National Conservatory, then considered the finest drama school in the world. This image is one of many street scenes by the Impressionist painter Jean Béraud (1849–1935).

ways bored her to tears or drove her to hysterical laughter. She read plays by the great French playwrights Racine and Molière. Her greatest inspiration came from Alexandre Dumas, the prolific French writer who had already written

The Count of Monte Cristo and *The Three Musketeers*, works that would become classics of Western literature. (Dumas and his son, also named Alexandre, were both noteworthy authors; the elder Dumas is referred to in French as Dumas *père*, i.e., "Dumas the father," and the younger as Dumas *fils*, "the son.") Realizing her potential, he called her "Little Star." A leading founder of Romanticism in literature, Dumas *père* was a mentor to the actress who would become the last, best example of the Romantic school of acting. Bernhardt responded to his intense coaching, watching as he brought characters to life with his gestures and his voice. Dumas found her voice exceptional, made to charm audiences; he called it "a spring that ripples and leaps over golden pebbles." (Skinner, 27–28)

Bernhardt's voice also charmed the audition committee at the Conservatory, and two of the distinguished teachers asked to have her in their classes. Once enrolled at the school, Bernhardt threw herself into her work, learning many more roles than were assigned to her and practicing diction exercises for hours on end. After two years of working hard and never missing a class, she was ready to graduate. There was great excitement among the graduates about the commencement competition, in which each student performed one scene of tragedy and one scene of comedy, competing for prizes awarded by the faculty. Bernhardt was not happy with the scenes assigned to her, but she was determined to win the competition anyway.

On the day of the competition, Judith insisted that her hairdresser arrange her daughter's unruly hair. After an hour and a half of suffering as the poor man tried every way possible to tame the mop (constantly protesting that the only way to manage it was to shave it off and let it grow in again), the struggling young actress escaped from his ministrations. She was horrified to find her golden halo weighed down with greasy pomade and pinned into sausage curls with five or six packets of pins. She began to weep with rage until her eyes were red, her nose swollen, and her voice thick and croaking.

When the time came to perform the tragic scene, Bernhardt did not recognize her own voice. Somehow she stumbled through the piece, curtsied, and walked off the stage to faint in the arms of Madame Guérard. She was not surprised to win no prize for this performance. Fortunately, there was an interval before the comedy competition. During that time she drank port wine and ate a sweet roll. Her hair loosened up a bit, and her will to win had returned. *Quand même* she would perform the comedy scene with skill and grace, and she did, winning second prize in that category. Second place, however, was never a happy option for Bernhardt, and for several days, she moped miserably around the house.

In the meantime, the Duc de Morny had again busied himself on her behalf. To her surprise and great joy, a letter arrived from the administrator-in-chief of the Comédie Française requesting an interview. The Comédie Française was the most important theater in France, and she was beside herself with pride and happiness.

DEBUT AT THE COMÉDIE FRANÇAISE

Bernhardt arrived for the interview in grand style—in a luxurious carriage borrowed from her aunt Rosine, complete with coachman and footman. She wore a cabbage-green dress with black velvet trim, a black grosgrain cloak, and a broad-brimmed straw hat. Her mother gave her a turquoise ring, and Madame Guérard lent her a frilly parasol.

Edouard Thierry, the administrator of the Comédie Française, signed Bernhardt as a *pensionnaire* at the pitifully small salary paid beginning actors at that time—a salary that would scarcely have paid for the carriage for an afternoon. Fortunately, she did not have to depend on her paycheck for support. She could live at her mother's and enjoy entertainment at her aunt's, such as the dinner party given by Aunt Rosine a few days after Bernhardt signed with the famous theater. In addition to the Duc de Morny, an illegitimate son of Napoleon was a guest, as was the composer Rossini, who accompanied Bernhardt on the piano as she recited a poem.

Determined to become a great actress, Bernhardt threw herself into learning the roles she would perform in the three debuts required by the theater. One day in August of 1862, when she saw her name on a yellow playbill announcing coming attractions, she stood transfixed, reading the words over and over: "*Iphigénie* by Racine. For the debut of Mademoiselle Sarah Bernhardt in the role of Iphigénie." It was hard to believe she was really going to appear in the greatest theater in France in the leading role of a play by the greatest French writer of tragedies.

Instead of the triumph Bernhardt had dreamed of, the debut was a disappointment thanks to an overwhelming case of stage fright. Standing in the wings waiting to go on, she was paralyzed with fear. One of her teachers from the Conservatory stood with her, encouraging her and finally pushing her onto the stage when she failed to hear her cue. She gabbled her lines and fled to her dressing room after the first act, feverishly undressing until she was reminded there were four more acts to the play. Scrawling a defiant "*Quand même!*" on her mirror in grease paint, she returned to play the remaining acts with all the courage she could muster.

The critics treated this performance with coolness, as they did her other appearances at the Française. None of the critics predicted a bright future for the young actress, and some thought she would soon disappear from the acting scene. For a time, thanks to an incident caused by her volatile temper, it seemed they might be right.

The interior of the Comédie Française, Paris, 1822. **The Comédie Française, "the House of Molière," was considered the most important theater in France; this is where Sarah Bernhardt saw her first play and fell in love with the theater. Through the connections of the Duc de Morny, a friend of her mother's, she received a request to interview with the theater, an opportunity with the potential to open many doors for an aspiring actress. Years later, she would become the star of the Française, and after that she would break with the theater completely.**

Bernhardt and her little sister Régina had formed a close bond, intensified by their mother's open preference for their sister Jeanne. At nine, Régina was a strange little girl. She rarely smiled or talked, but she adored Sarah and wanted to go everywhere with her. Like Sarah, she had a fiery temper and sometimes threw spectacular tantrums enhanced by obscene language she had picked up from the servants. Bernhardt often took her lonely little sister to rehearsals with her, and the unpredictable child had always behaved well. When it was time for the theater's annual birthday celebration in honor of Molière, its founder, Régina begged to go along, and Bernhardt consented to take her.

The celebration was a solemn ritual. Before the reading of poems to Molière and the performing of scenes from his plays, the actors lined up in stately procession to lay palm fronds on the poet's bust. Holding Régina's hand, Bernhardt awaited her turn in line behind Madame Nathalie, a formidable veteran actress of gigantic proportions. For the ceremony Madame Nathalie wore a voluminous purple robe with a three-foot train. At her turn to deposit her palm frond, Madame Nathalie started forward majestically—only to be jerked to a sudden stop.

Turning to find Régina standing on her train, she grabbed the child and shoved her with such force into a stucco pillar with a sharp edge that it cut a gash in Régina's forehead. Blood streaming down her face, Régina screamed that she hadn't meant to stand on the train and the big, fat cow had no right to push her. Springing to her little sister's defense, Bernhardt slapped Madame Nathalie so hard she toppled to the floor. It was a blow that rocked the House of Molière and resounded throughout Paris.

The press had a field day describing the audacity of the first-year *pensionnaire* who dared to strike a *sociétaire*, or senior member, of the venerable acting establishment. Cartoons picturing the scene ran in the papers, and "The Slap" was the talk of the town. It was the beginning of 60 years of notoriety that would accompany Sarah Bernhardt's career.

In the meantime, Monsieur Thierry called the impudent actress to his office. The seriousness of her crime was explained to her, and she was ordered to apologize publicly to Madame

Nathalie and pay a large fine. She would apologize only after Madame Nathalie apologized to Régina, Bernhardt told him. Hoping she would change her mind, Thierry kept her on for several weeks, but Madame Nathalie insisted that Bernhardt be given no parts until she made a public apology. This Bernhardt repeatedly refused to do, and her contract was terminated. It would be almost a decade before she would again appear at the Comédie Française.

DIFFICULT TIMES

After her abrupt departure from the Comédie Française, the details of the next four years of Bernhardt's life are unclear. Her family and friends told her she had thrown away her chance of becoming a respected actress. Because she didn't have the personality or the will to become a courtesan like her mother and aunt, her best course was to marry a wealthy man. Everyone except Bernhardt agreed. Various suitors with large fortunes, some of them ancient lechers, were urged on her, but she would have none of them. However, all accounts of her life, including her own, say it was at this time that she began taking and discarding lovers. Accounts of her love affairs were probably exaggerated by biographers or by Bernhardt herself, who delighted in shocking people.

At 18, she had not given up on herself as an actress. Through the influence of one of her mother's friends, she got a job at the Gymnase, a popular theater that presented light comedies. Bernhardt appeared in a few trivial plays without attracting any attention; then she was cast as a giddy Russian princess named Dumchinka. The play was silly, and her mother told her that her acting was ridiculous.

In despair, Bernhardt sent a note of resignation to the manager of the Gymnase and went on a trip. Where she went is a matter of dispute; she may have gone to Spain, where she claims to have met bullfighters and been wined and dined by noble grandees. Her trip ended in Belgium, where she had an affair with Henri, Prince de Ligne, a handsome nobleman whom she said was the one great love of her life. At any rate, she returned to Paris pregnant with his child.

Bernhardt had enjoyed her taste of independence immensely, and using part of the dowry left to her by her father, she moved to a small flat on the Rue Duphot, taking her sister Régina and the faithful Madame Guérard with her. On December 22, 1864, her son, Maurice, was born. She loved her only child with all the fierce passion of her nature, and from that time on, no matter what else happened in her life, he remained its focus.

AT THE ODÉON

The Odéon Theater on the Left Bank was the second most important theater in Paris. Less bound by tradition than the Comédie Française, it constantly tried out new plays and presented fresh versions of the classics. To have a job at this excellent theater was an honor. Desperately in need of a way to support herself and her son, Bernhardt applied to the French minister of arts to help her get an interview with Felix Duquesnel, one of the managers of the Odéon. The minister lectured her on her past behavior, telling her that she had earned a reputation as an unstable, temperamental actress. She shed floods of tears and promised to reform, and he gave her the letter of introduction.

She and Duquesnel were charmed with each other. The gallant young manager said of their first meeting: "I beheld before me the most ideally charming creature one can dream of. . . . She was not pretty, she was better than pretty." (Skinner, 53) Bernhardt was pleased to sign a contract with the Odéon for 150 francs a month.

Her first roles in her new job were not especially suitable for her, and she received little attention. Then, in a translation of Shakespeare's *King Lear* she scored a big success as Cordelia, the misunderstood, tenderhearted daughter, and critics began to take notice of her talent. Another breakthrough came with her appearance as the female lead in *Kean,* a play by Dumas *père* about the famous English Shakespearean actor Edmund Kean. Dumas was delighted to see his protégé perform to acclaim in his play. He puffed his way backstage to kiss her hand repeatedly and vowed he would write a new play especially for her. He died two years later before he could do so.

Bernhardt also starred successfully in two plays by the novelist George Sand. Sand, then in her sixties, wrote to the young actress to thank her for performing like an angel, and a warm friendship developed between the two strong-willed women. Bernhardt greatly admired the famous authoress, who defied convention by wearing men's clothes, smoking cigars, and advocating and practicing free love. Talking with Madame Sand as the writer sat in her dressing room smoking or strolling with her in the Luxembourg Gardens, Bernhardt confided her ambition to be the greatest actress in the world.

Sarah Bernhardt called herself a "*traqueuse*"—someone subject to acute attacks of *le trac*, or stage fright. In her early days of acting, she was embarrassed to speak so loudly in front of so many silent people and would turn beet-red when she met a spectator's eyes. In January of 1869, during the seventh or eighth performance of the hugely successful *Le Passant*, she was so overcome by stage fright that she told her grandmother that she would have to quit the stage. She didn't think she could live up to the expectations of her fans. Her grandmother reminded her of her goal to become the best actress in the world and called her "a bad soldier." Bernhardt resolved to continue her career even though stage fright often made a "martyr" of her. (*Memoirs*, 80–81)

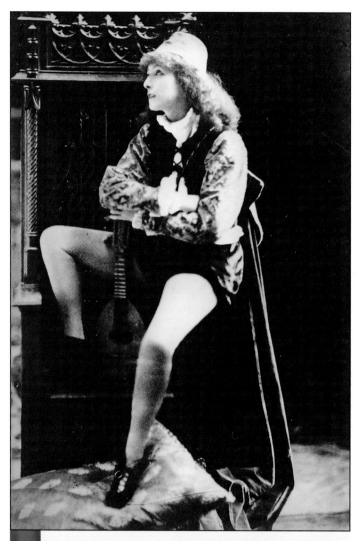

Bernhardt as Zanetto. After an incident of behavior earned Bernhardt the reputation of instability, she pleaded for an opportunity to audition for the Odéon, the second most important theater in Paris at the time. Her charms landed her a contract with the theater and the role of Zanetto, "a strolling boy troubadour," which established her reputation of irresistible appeal with the public and the press.

The production that brought Sarah rave reviews and convinced skeptics of her undeniable ability was a one-act drama in which she played the part of a boy troubadour. The poet François Coppée wrote *Le Passant* as a romantic love duet. The plot is simple: Sylvia, a Florentine beauty, bemoans the fact that she is unable to love because she has a heart of stone. Zanetto, a strolling boy troubadour, appears in search of a woman named Sylvia whose loveliness enthralls all who meet her. He falls under her spell and begs to remain with her forever as her minstrel slave. She gently turns him down although he has melted her heart, and he goes on his way to sing his songs even more poignantly because of their meeting. Sylvia, for the first time in her life, weeps.

Le Passant, which opened on January 14, 1868, was scheduled for only a few performances; it ran for 150. The public and the press found Bernhardt's Zanetto irresistible; the little lute player became as popular as Peter Pan. Critics praised the "delicate and tender charm" of her interpretation, her eloquent grace, and her crystal voice. It became the play to see for the aristocracy, as well as for the intellectuals and students of the Left Bank. After a command performance at the Tuileries, the emperor sent Sarah a magnificent brooch with the imperial initials in diamonds. At 24, Sarah Bernhardt had arrived.

Her blossoming career came to an abrupt halt in mid-July of 1870, when Napoleon III declared war on Prussia. It was a terrible mistake; in a few weeks, the emperor surrendered his sword to Prussia's William I, and on September 4 the Bonapartes were deposed. The Second Empire was finished, but the war continued and the Siege of Paris began. Theaters closed their doors, as actors went off to war. Bernhardt saw her family—Judith, Jeanne, Régina, and Maurice—off on a train bound for the safety of Le Havre. Back in her empty apartment, she pondered what she could do for the war effort. If she could get permission, she decided she would open a hospital in the Odéon.

First, she would need to obtain permission from the prefect of police. When she called at his office, she was delighted to find that the prefect was the Comte de Keratry, an old friend she had met at her mother's. Wasting no time, she asked for a permit to open a convalescent hospital and brought out her list. She needed bread, milk, meat, vegetables, sugar, potatoes, eggs, and coffee. Keratry readily agreed to supply everything on the list. When she noticed his luxurious fur-lined coat and asked for it for one of her soldiers, he gave her that also.

Bernhardt used her persuasive talents to solicit donations from other friends and family. The Rothschilds sent brandy and wine; a neighbor sent a hundred tins of sardines, sacks of rice, and barrels of raisins; another friend, a flour merchant, sent sacks of flour; the chocolate manufacturer Menier sent 500 pounds of chocolate; and the Dutch ambassador contributed lint and linen.

Bernhardt's own cook managed the immense coal stove, and the cook's husband was employed to drive the horse-drawn ambulance. Madame Guérard and Marie Colombier, a fellow actress, served with Bernhardt as nurses. They cared for hundreds of wounded in the hospital. When extreme cold weather struck Paris in January of 1871, she ordered the props and the seats of the Odéon chopped up for firewood. People were starving in the streets. Dogs, cats, and animals at the zoo were used as food, and Bernhardt often gave her own rations to a hungry soldier.

When the bombardment of Paris began on December 27, and the hospital flag on the Odéon became a target for Prussian gunners, she ordered the patients transferred to the cellars. When the cellars proved uninhabitable because of broken pipes and hungry rats, she sent the sickest patients to another hospital and rented an empty apartment, where she and Madame Guérard nursed the rest back to health.

For once, Sarah Bernhardt was not playing a role.

Sincerely and passionately patriotic, she worked heroically with all her tremendous energy and resources to care for "her soldiers." The French government recognized her effort by awarding her a well-deserved gold medal for her work during the siege.

Rising Star

1870–1879

You must have . . . charm to reach the pinnacle. It is made of everything and of nothing, the striving will, the look, the walk, the proportions of the body, the sound of the voice, the ease of the gestures. It is not at all necessary to be handsome or to be pretty; all that is needful is charm.

—Sarah Bernhardt, *The Art of the Theatre* (1924)

Acting is the expression of a neurotic impulse. It's a bum's life. . . . The principal benefit acting has afforded me is the money to pay for my psychoanalysis.

—Marlon Brando, quoted in Gary Carey's
Marlon Brando: The Only Contender (1985)

POLITICAL UPHEAVAL

Toward the end of the siege of Paris, Bernhardt received word that her mother had moved the family from the safety of Le Havre to Hamburg, Germany. Judith thought the family

A portrait of the immortal Sarah Bernhardt by Georges Clairin. It was in the salon of her apartment in the Rue de Rome that Bernhardt posed for this painting by the artist Georges Clairin. Bernhardt appreciated the encouragement she received from Clairin in her own endeavors with painting, and the two became close. This portrait has been described as the "epitome of Romanticism" and is said to have inspired many women to commission similar works starring themselves. Bernhardt kept this painting in prominent display throughout her life.

would be safer in the land of the conqueror, but Bernhardt was horrified and set out immediately to rescue them. All her powers of persuasion were necessary to obtain permission to travel to Hamburg, and the trip itself was a dangerous nightmare. Traveling by coal train, garbage wagon, and peasant cart, she collected her family, and holding Maurice tightly in her arms, brought them all back to France.

They endured the ghastly civil uprising, as the people of France attempted to establish a commune, which was brutally crushed by the French army. From the relative safety of the suburbs, Bernhardt, along with hundreds of other refugees, watched as their beloved city burned. The Communards set fire to the Palais de Justice, the Palace of the Tuileries, the grand Hôtel de Ville, and many theaters and churches. More than 20,000 men, women and children died in the bloody holocaust.

RUY BLAS

At the end of May 1871, the Commune ended and the stage was set for the Third Republic to begin. Discouraged by the devastation of her country, Bernhardt returned to her still smoky apartment in a dismal frame of mind. Lying on her fur-covered chaise lounge with the draperies pulled, she gave herself up to melancholy until the day she was summoned to work at the Odéon. The newly refurbished theater was back in business and in need of its popular actress to start the season. She appeared in several plays that were well received; then came the opportunity that would make her a superstar.

Victor Hugo, France's great poet and novelist, had just returned to his country after nearly 20 years of political exile. Through the years, his *Notre Dame de Paris* and *Les Misérables* had become classics, and Giuseppe Verdi had made Hugo's story "The King Amuses Himself" into the much-loved opera *Rigoletto*. Hugo returned to his homeland a hero, and audiences were eager to see his works performed. Bernhardt was filled with pride when he chose her to play Doña Maria, the unhappy queen of Spain in the revival of his play *Ruy Blas*.

When Hugo himself attended rehearsals, Bernhardt was captivated by his wit and charm. Meanwhile, critics were captivated by her performance. Dressed in shimmering white brocade shot with silver thread and a silver crown on her head, she was an unforgettable work of art, they declared. They could scarcely find words to praise "the grace of her gestures, the beauty of her voice, and her superb declamation of Hugo's verse." (Gold, 93) The opening night audience, her "beloved monster," was also wildly enthusiastic. After the final curtain, the admirers who jammed her dressing room included England's Prince of Wales and Victor Hugo, who knelt before her, kissing her hands and saying, "*Merci! Merci!*" When she finally made her way through the delirious crowds outside the theater, frenzied students replaced the horses of her carriage and ran with it through the streets to her apartment.

RETURN TO THE COMÉDIE FRANÇAISE

Ruy Blas was the outstanding hit of the Paris season; everyone talked about it and about Sarah Bernhardt. When Emile Perrin, the director of the Comédie Française, invited her to sign a contract with France's leading theater, she knew she had arrived. The offer was, in effect, an apology for her dismissal from the theater house ten years earlier. The salary Perrin offered was higher and the prestige was greater than at the Odéon, so although her contract still had a year to run, she signed with the Française. This unethical behavior cost her 6,000 francs in fines and an ugly break with the directors of the Odéon, who considered her ungrateful for the opportunity they had given her to become a star.

Bernhardt's return to the national theater of France was not easy—for the theater or for Bernhardt. Some of the established actors at the venerable theater did not welcome the addition of this volatile actress who was known for attracting questionable publicity. The autocratic Perrin had difficulty dealing with Bernhardt's own autocratic ways. In *My Double Life* (177) she says, "M. Perrin, a man of superior intelligence whom I remember with great affection, was horribly dictatorial and so was I." She admits that she delighted in driving him into frenzies, so that he would turn red, sputter, and pull his hat on and off "fifteen times in fifteen minutes."

For his part, Perrin had final control because he could refuse roles that she requested. At first he cast her in roles that were not suited to her talents. His favorite actress was Sophie

Croizette, Bernhardt's opposite. He much preferred to give the best roles to this tall, agreeable young woman rather than to the demanding Bernhardt, whom he called "the rebel." Bernhardt's reaction to being assigned an inferior role was to upstage Croizette whenever she could. The two women had actually been friends for many years and remained friends, despite exaggerated reports of their rivalry. For her part, Bernhardt didn't mind the rumors; after all, the publicity attracted people to the theater to see the "rivals" perform.

The press and public opinion of the increasingly famous actress ran hot and cold. One day, stories would praise her acting talent, her unique voice, her beguiling looks; the next day, cartoons would lampoon her skinny figure, her wild hair, and her outrageous public behavior. Every tidbit of information, fact or fiction, was analyzed and eagerly repeated.

Her apartment in the Rue de Rome was a favorite topic of gossip. The main salon, filled with antiques, Persian carpeted floors covered in bear, lion and tiger skin rugs, had red damask walls barely visible through the paintings, Japanese fans, and other knickknacks hung on them. Every vacant space was filled with huge potted plants and hothouse flowers, and first-time visitors were often alarmed by her menagerie, which included dogs of all sizes, parrots, and an occasional exotic animal. Dominating the salon was her divan on its raised platform. Oriental canopies upheld by velvet-covered spears hung over the enormous satin pillows and piles of fur covers strewn over it. On this divan, she posed for her famous portrait painted by Georges Clairin, a well-known painter who became her lifelong friend. The picture was the epitome of romanticism. She is shown reclined against the exotic background of the divan, wearing a flowing white gown with a snow-white Russian wolfhound at her feet. Her expression is dreamy and mysterious. The picture was exhibited at a Paris salon, where crowds flocked to view it, and many Parisian ladies attempted to copy the pose when receiving gentlemen callers in their own homes.

Bernhardt in her salon. The main salon in Bernhardt's apartment in the Rue de Rome was a most appropriate expression of her elaborate and dramatic tastes. Filled with antiques, wild animal skins, an exotic treasure in nearly every available space, and a virtual menagerie of animal companions, the room could easily alarm guests not accustomed to the actress's extravagant tendencies.

The glamorous flow of Bernhardt's daily life was profoundly interrupted in 1874 by the death of her sister Régina. Bernhardt's younger sister had become like a daughter to her, and she nursed Régina tenderly day and night—to such a degree that Régina's doctor had to forbid Bernhardt to share Régina's bed. The bedroom was too small to accommodate a second bed, so Bernhardt had her own coffin, the coffin that their mother had given to her, fitted out with quilts and installed beside her sister's bed. It was an act of concern and practicality, but it was publicized as another Bernhardt perversity. When Régina finally died, Bernhardt was heartbroken.

OTHER ARTISTIC TALENTS

Bernhardt's drive to create art sometimes surpassed the amount of work she received from the theater, and when it did so, it expressed itself in other ways. Once, for example, she took up sculpture. As always, she threw herself into this new venture wholeheartedly. She took lessons, rented a studio, and worked long hours, forgetting to stop for meals or to go to the theater until her maid came to summon her. Her scandalous sculpting costume consisted of white silk trousers, a white satin blouse with white lace neck ruffle, and a long tie of white tulle. When a photographer took a picture of her in this outfit and made the picture into postcards, the management of the Comédie Française was outraged at her audacity to wear men's pants in public. Her fans were delighted, though, and they bought the postcards as fast as stores could stock them.

Bernhardt achieved a gratifying amount of success for her sculpting efforts. Her busts of well-known people and her other pieces were exhibited at salons and sold for respectable prices. Her bust of her sister Régina won a prize at an important exhibition. At about this same time, Bernhardt also began painting. She was an enthusiastic painter, encouraged and instructed by Clairin and the equally famous Gustave Doré, but she never won as much recognition in this field as she did in sculpting.

Bernhardt's enthusiasm appeared again when she decided to build a private home. She became deeply involved in the process, terrifying her friends by climbing on the scaffolding to dizzying heights and constantly offering advice to the carpenters, masons, and plasterers. The inside of the house was decorated with furnishings from the apartment, plus a flamboyant array of new acquisitions. Various artist friends painted some of the walls, with mixed results. Calling the house her "folly," she blithely dismissed the enormous cost. In addition, her extravagant lifestyle, which required two carriages, eight servants, and constant lavish entertainments, added to her large burden of debt.

PHÈDRE AND *HERNANI*

During her long acting career, Bernhardt was fortunate to have several outstanding leading men. Invariably, the press and the public looked for romantic connections, even where none existed. With Jean Mounet-Sully, however, they may have underrated the intensity of the offstage relationship between the handsome, virile actor and the fragile, very feminine actress. Bernhardt and Mounet-Sully appeared together in numerous plays to great acclaim, and Perrin was pressured by the press and the public to continue casting the couple together. Their greatest success came when they were cast as leads in Racine's *Phèdre.*

On December 21, 1874, the Française mounted a production of *Phèdre* to commemorate Racine's birthday. The role of Phaedra demands extraordinary acting from any actress brave enough to attempt it. The powerful story involves a passionate, cursed woman who falls in love with her husband's son, eventually causes the son's death, and commits suicide. The brilliant French actress Rachel, whom Bernhardt knew only by reputation, was considered to have been the ideal interpreter of the role, and her performance was the touchstone by which all other actresses were measured in the part. Perrin had originally cast another actress for the performance, and it was only because that woman had a violent argument with him and left the cast that Bernhardt was called in.

Luckily, Bernhardt had performed minor roles in the play and had studied the role of Phaedra in acting school. Still, the undertaking was tremendous—to perfect the role's gestures and speeches in only three days. It helped that Mounet-Sully was cast opposite her as the love object, Hippolytus. Despite an incipient attack of stage fright, Bernhardt gave a dazzling performance that won a thunderous ovation from the audience and rave reviews from critics. It was the first of many triumphs in the role. In Skinner's words, "Over the years Sarah Bernhardt as Phèdre was to become a sort of national institution which

Bernhardt in Jean Racine's *Phèdre.* The role of Phaedra was considered an intimidating one, for an exemplary standard had been set by the famous French actress Rachel. When Bernhardt first attempted the part, she did so with only three days to prepare, filling in at the last minute for an actress who had left the cast due to a charged dispute with the director. Her performance received rave reviews from critics and audiences alike, though, and over the years, the role would become one of her greatest legacies.

the French claimed as uniquely their own, along with Notre Dame and the Eiffel Tower." (107) Even though her portrayal of the heroine in *La Dame aux Camélias* came to have greater popular appeal, Phaedra has been called Bernhardt's most artistic performance.

The Française scored a major hit in the 1877–1878 season with Victor Hugo's *Hernani*, starring Bernhardt and Mounet-Sully. Bernhardt played Doña Sol, a noblewoman in love with the bandit Hernani, played by Mounet-Sully. In the play's emotional last act, when it is revealed that Hernani is doomed, the lovers form a suicide pact and drink from a vial of poison. Bernhardt's electrifying performance and the sight of the dead lovers in each other's arms overwhelmed the audience, and it also overwhelmed the author. The day after the opening, Bernhardt received a gift and a note from Victor Hugo (Gold, 140):

> Madame:
>
> You were great, and you were charming; you moved me, the old warrior, and at a certain moment when the public cheered, enchanted and overcome by emotion, I wept. The tear which you drew from me belongs to you. I place it at your feet.

The "tear" that Victor Hugo sent was a pear-shaped diamond suspended from a delicate gold bracelet. In time, many Parisians came to refer to Bernhardt affectionately as Doña Sol.

HOT-AIR BALLOON SCRAPE

In the mid-nineteenth century, Henri Giffard, a French engineer, combined a three-horsepower steam engine with a propeller to drive a balloon through the air at a speed of about five miles per hour. Giffard kept a captive balloon moored in the gardens of the Tuileries, where the public could come to experience the feeling of soaring in the air.

For a small fee, Giffard took customers up in the hanging basket to a height of 500 meters. Sarah Bernhardt was a frequent visitor to the tethered airship, but she yearned for a real flying experience, so she persuaded Giffard to arrange a flight for her. Working with Louis Godard, a young balloonist, Giffard prepared a special airship for the actress; on the side of the bag, in gold letters, was the ship's name—the *Doña Sol*.

Bernhardt invited her friend Clairin to accompany her. She wore a long, trailing white cashmere dress for the flight, with a fur-trimmed jacket, a gossamer scarf, and polished riding boots. Clairin wore a smart suit and a top hat. In addition to Clairin's sketchpad, their supplies included a telescope and a picnic hamper. When the passengers were in the gondola, Godard freed the anchor and vaulted aboard. He tossed sandbags over the side, and the *Doña Sol* set sail over Paris. As they drifted over the Père Lachaise Cemetery, Bernhardt tossed flowers in the direction of Régina's and Judith's graves, the latter having died two years before.

Bernhardt capitalized on her balloon caper by writing a delightful book about it. Profusely illustrated with charming pictures by Clairin, the book sold well. The story's narrator is a chair that accompanies the actress, Doña Sol, on her ride. It was advertised as a children's book, but adults also loved reading Bernhardt's playful spoofing of the exaggerated rumors that circulated about her. "They say of Doña Sol," the chair reports, "that she feasts on dainties made of lizard tails, eats peacocks' brains sautéed in monkey fat, and plays croquet with human skulls topped with Louis XIV wigs." (*The Divine Sarah*, 145–146)

Bernhardt and Clairin were euphoric. They recited poetry, sang songs, ate *foie gras* sandwiches, and drank champagne, toasting the future of aviation and artists past and present. Looking up at the low-flying craft with its unmistakable name and the equally unmistakable figure with streaming scarves and veils, Parisians were entranced; the notable exception was Perrin. A friend pointed out the craft to him, and Perrin, watching his star sailing above his head, was livid.

As night fell, Godard opened hissing valves and threw guide ropes overboard. Five men caught the ropes as they came to ground near a small railroad station. The adventure had ended. After a tedious wait, Bernhardt caught a train for Paris, arriving at her destination in the middle of the night.

The next day Perrin called Bernhardt into his office and reprimanded her. By leaving Paris without special permission, he informed her, she had broken one of the strict rules of the Comédie Française. Furthermore, Perrin raged, her antics disgraced France's national theater. He demanded that she pay a fine of 1,000 francs for the infraction, but Bernhardt laughed in his face. The rule was ridiculous, she said, and she could hardly have stopped the winds from carrying the balloon out of bounds. She declared that she had no intention of paying the fine; she would resign from the Française before she would pay it.

Perrin knew well that Sarah Bernhardt was the principal attraction of the Comédie Française and that her public would follow her to another theater. Moreover, the company was preparing to travel to England for its first foreign appearance, and London's Gaiety Theatre would cancel the contract if Bernhardt were not in the troupe. He was again forced to yield to his rebellious star, and he hastily backed down.

Bernhardt's Conquest of London

1879–1880

What would life be without art? Science prolongs life. To consist of what—eating, drinking, and sleeping? What is the good of living longer if it is only a matter of satisfying the requirements that sustain life? All this is nothing without the charm of art.

—Sarah Bernhardt, *The Art of the Theatre* (1924)

EDWARD JARRETT, IMPRESARIO

A few days before the company of the Comédie Française departed for England, Bernhardt received a caller who would change her life. On the day of his visit, she was absorbed in painting and told her manservant to send the uninvited guest away. But Edward Jarrett had traveled from London with the intention of seeing Sarah Bernhardt, and he was not a man easily dissuaded. Disturbed by the sound of an argument, Bernhardt finally appeared to chase the intruder away herself.

Sarah Bernhardt in the role of Froufrou. **Expanding beyond the Comédie Française, Bernhardt began to accept contracts to appear in London and elsewhere, and her popularity increased exponentially. The Gaiety Theatre in London gave her the opportunity to select her own plays and to choose the actors who would perform in them. The role of Froufrou was most appropriate for Bernhardt, as the emotional nature of the part showcased her talents. The costume pictured here was among the many that Bernhardt provided herself; she was very particular about the look and construction of her costumes, and she often paid great sums of money to have them made to her specifications.**

In the doorway of her studio, she saw a tall man with "clear, hard eyes, silver hair, and a well-groomed beard." After apologizing for the intrusion, he admired her paintings and sculptures so enthusiastically that she became willing to sit and discuss the purpose of his visit. He introduced himself and told her that he had come to make her fortune. He asked her if she would like to go to America. Her reply was vehement: "Never! Never! Never!" (*My Double Life*, 200)

"Oh, well," he soothed, "don't get upset." Handing her his card, he told her not to lose it. As he was leaving, Jarrett asked if she wanted to make lots of money while in London with the Française. To this, Bernhardt, who always needed money, eagerly replied, "Yes!" Before Jarrett left, she had signed a contract to perform in private drawing rooms in London for fees greater than her salary at the Française.

Perrin and other members of the Comédie Française committee were unhappy over arrangements by Bernhardt and several other company members to give these private performances. There was nothing they could do about it, though, but complain. In the meantime, Jarrett happily sent notices to the papers, including the London *Times*, announcing that Sarah Bernhardt's repertoire would include "comedies, sketches, one-act plays, and monologues," especially written for her, suitable for performing without scenery or props in the drawing rooms of the "best" society. (Gold, 148)

This agreement marked the beginning of a long and profitable relationship. Jarrett, who called himself an "impresario," was the outstanding public-relations manager of his day. He had offices in London, New York, and Paris and worldwide connections in music and the theater. He arranged the tours that would indeed make fortunes for both of them. Bernhardt was charmed by, and perhaps in awe of, this formidable man, who called her bluff when she threw tantrums or tried to back out of arrangements he had made to promote her performances. She called him "the Ferocious Gentleman" and "the Terrible Mr. Garrett," but they respected each other and worked closely together for seven years, until Jarrett's sudden death in 1886.

THE ARRIVAL ABROAD

Crowds of fans gathered at the dock to wish the actors from France's national theater a *bon voyage* as they departed for their first trip abroad. That was to be expected, but what surprised and delighted the troupe was the enthusiastic crowd waiting to greet them when they disembarked at Folkestone. Thanks to Jarrett's advance publicity, the English knew that in France Sarah Bernhardt's fame rivaled that of Joan of Arc.

It soon became clear that she was the one most of them had come to see. Not all the other players were pleased with the attention paid to her, as hands reached out to touch her and offer her bouquets of flowers. "Soon they'll be making you a carpet of flowers," a jealous colleague remarked. (*My Double Life*, 204) "Here it is," cried a tall young man, throwing an armful of white lilies in her path. He led the crowd escorting the troupe to the train in crying, "*Vive Sarah Bernhardt!*" ("Long live Sarah Bernhardt!") The dashing young man was Oscar Wilde, the Irish dramatist, poet, socialite, and wit. He and Bernhardt had met in Paris a few years earlier. During her stay in London, he sent her flowers and dinner invitations, praised her performances extravagantly, and wrote a sonnet to her. They remained friends throughout his life, and they enjoyed each other's company whenever their paths crossed.

A charming house in Chester Square had been rented for Bernhardt and Madame Guérard, who remained Bernhardt's constant companion, for their six-week stay in London. It included an attractive garden, elegant furnishings, and an efficient staff. The hall and drawing room were filled with flowers from well-wishers and stacks of correspondence: welcome notes, requests for autographs, and invitations to tea, meals, and various parties.

The morning after their arrival, Jarrett told her that 37 reporters would be arriving very soon, eager to interview her. She asked to see them all together, but he insisted that she talk with them separately as a courtesy to the various publications. If not, he warned, she might get bad press. Because she spoke English poorly and the reporters spoke poor French, Jarrett translated questions and answers. The first question was invariably about her opinion of London. As she had seen only the train station and her house and had never been one to suffer foolish questions patiently, Bernhardt refused to answer. Jarrett had no such scruples. She later learned from the newspapers that she was enthusiastic about the beauty of London and already familiar with many of its monuments. Fortunately, with time, these statements would prove to be true.

That afternoon a duchess came to call, and that night Bernhardt dined at the home of a countess. The next day she went for a carriage ride on Rotten Row in Hyde Park. It was a beautiful day, and Bernhardt was enchanted by the flowers, the multicolored parasols of the exquisitely dressed ladies, the children riding ponies, the elegant carriages, the footmen in powdered wigs, and the horses decorated with flowers.

THE DIVINE SARAH IN LONDON

The Comédie Française gave its first London performance on June 2, 1879. When the curtain rose to reveal the more than 50 members of the company dressed in their costumes, the audience applauded with great enthusiasm. Bernhardt's assignment was to appear in the second act of *Phèdre*, which was to be sandwiched between two full-length plays by Molière. The English audience was familiar with the great Rachel's classic performance in the role of Phaedra, and Bernhardt knew the viewers were waiting to compare.

Bernhardt sometimes said that there were two kinds of stage fright that plagued her: the paralyzing kind and the maddening kind. The former froze her tongue and body, and the latter made her actions frenzied. While waiting for the first Molière play to finish, Bernhardt was overcome with the worst stage fright she had ever experienced—this time, the maddening kind. Rather than damaging her performance, however, her fear

Bernhardt in a production of *Phèdre*. Throughout her career, Bernhardt returned again and again to the challenging role of Phaedra, and again and again she achieved unparalleled success. In the play, Phaedra, the wife of Theseus and the daughter of the cursed King Minos of Crete, falls in love with Hippolytus, her stepson. This photograph of Bernhardt as the queen with Oenone, her nurse and confidante, shows Bernhardt's moving portrayal of the character's struggle with a passion she cannot control.

intensified the anguish of the play's tortured heroine. "I suffered, I wept, I implored, I cried," she said, "and all of it was real; my suffering was horrible; the tears that flowed were burning and bitter. I implored Hippolyte for the love that was killing me, and the arms that I stretched out to Mounet-Sully were the arms of Phaedra, tense with the cruel longing to embrace." (Richardson, 79)

The audience was transfixed by her performance. They *believed* the tragedy. When the act ended and Bernhardt, obviously faint with exhaustion, stood on the stage supported by Mounet-Sully, the crowd stood and cheered in an ovation unusual for British audiences. The critics were equally impressed. Rachel's Phaedra may have been more somber and intense, they said, but Bernhardt's was more womanlike and sympathetic. This performance was a defining moment in Bernhardt's career.

On Jarrett's advice, she had brought along nine of her sculptures and sixteen of her oil paintings for exhibition and sale. The exhibition was held in a Piccadilly art gallery; about 100 invitations were sent out, but nearly 400 people from the world of the arts and high society attended. The Prince and Princess of Wales were there, as was Prime Minister William Gladstone. Ten pictures and six pieces of sculpture sold for high prices, making a nice profit for both Bernhardt and Jarrett.

Bernhardt was in the limelight again at a charitable event called the French Fête, which was organized to raise funds for the French Hospital in London. Her stall, stocked with Bernhardt memorabilia such as plates, photographs, portrait copies, and plaques, was the center of attention—especially after the Prince of Wales lingered there. Making full use of her fame, Bernhardt repeatedly increased the prices of the commemorative pieces and harangued her admirers until she raised a record amount for the hospital.

Her love of animals also won her a considerable amount of celebrity in London. Although she had already collected a small menagerie consisting of three dogs, a parrot, and a monkey named Darwin, she decided to spend some of her earnings from the art exhibition on more pets. During some free time from the playbill at the Gaiety, she and a few friends traveled by train to visit the Cross Zoo at Liverpool. She admired the lion cubs and baby elephant, but she realized they might grow too large to be house pets and settled on a young cheetah and a large wolfhound.

Mr. Cross, the owner of the zoo, threw in seven gratis chameleons for his distinguished visitor. One of these was a rare specimen with protruding eyes that were frequently crossed. Bernhardt was so charmed with this homely beast that she went to a jeweler and had a gold chain fastened around its neck so that she could pin the end of the chain to her lapel as an ornament.

Back at her house in London, neither the preexisting menagerie nor the domestic staff was as delighted as Bernhardt with the new pets. Madame Guérard fled shrieking into the house, and the butler recoiled in horror as the cheetah bounded joyously from its cage. The dogs howled in terror; the parrot shrieked with excitement; Darwin shook his cage and emitted ear-splitting squeals. Chester Square had never seen or heard anything like it. "All the windows opened, and above the wall of my garden more than twenty heads appeared, curious, trembling, furious," Bernhardt recorded. (*My Double Life*, 221) She and visiting friends, who included Georges Clairin and Gustave Doré, collapsed in hysterical laughter.

By the next day, the bedlam at Chester Square had become the talk of the town. Although the manager of the Comédie Française admitted it had been a funny scene, he warned Bernhardt to stop acting like a madwoman before she caused serious damage to the reputation of the company. London scandal sheets latched onto this latest incident to report that the French actress had wild animals running loose in her gardens. (They also claimed that for a shilling Bernhardt would pose dressed as a man, that she smoked cigars on the balcony of her home, and that she was taking boxing lessons and had broken two of her boxing teacher's teeth.)

BERNHARDT'S BREAK WITH THE COMÉDIE FRANÇAISE
The French press was quick to repeat the outrageous stories and criticized her for mixing commerce with art and for behavior that was unbecoming in a member of the House of Molière (as the Comédie Française was sometimes called).

Parting ways with the Comédie Française, circa 1880. In response to reports of "scandalous behavior," the director of the Comédie Française forced Bernhardt to perform in a role she despised, resulting in an unfortunate performance and wave of bad reviews, the first of her career. Shortly thereafter and around the time of this photograph, Bernhardt sent word to the Française that she intended to resign from the company—determined to make this one round of negative reviews her last.

Indignant, Bernhardt sent a long, expensive telegram to the Parisian newspaper *Le Figaro*, denying the "stupid" stories circulating about her and offering to resign as a member of the Française rather than have people think she lacked respect for it. Her telegram was published in the paper and created an uproar in Paris. A delegation from the Comédie Française called on her and begged her not to resign, and Perrin sent a wire assuring her of his admiration and devotion. She tabled her thoughts of resigning and finished her first London season as she had begun it, to packed houses.

The French public soon forgave her transgressions, and viewers rewarded her with thunderous applause when she appeared at the annual celebration of Molière's birthday. The French press, however, remained hostile. Perrin treated his rebellious star in the same bullying manner as before, even though she had fine successes in the 1879–1880 season as the queen in *Ruy Blas* and Doña Sol in *Hernani*. In the spring of 1880, Perrin cast her in a role she hated, in a play she despised. When she begged him to delay the opening for a week, claiming illness, he forced her to perform. As a result, she performed badly, and the critics mercilessly panned the play and the acting. After reading every bad review, she wrote to Perrin telling him:

> This is my first failure at the Comédie and it shall be my last. I warned you on the day of the dress rehearsal and you ignored my warning. I keep my word. When you receive this letter I shall have left Paris. Be so kind, Monsieur Administrator, as to accept my immediate resignation. . . . (Skinner, 141)

She sent copies of the letter to the two leading French papers and retreated to Le Havre to wait out the furor she knew the action would cause.

Her contract with the Française committed her to another 15 years with the company, and the Française immediately began a lawsuit for breach of contract. The suit resulted in the loss of money she had invested in the theater's pension fund and a fine of 100,000 francs. The suit would remain in litigation for the next two decades. Bernhardt would settle it in 1900 by allowing the Française, whose building had been burned, to use her theater while she was on tour.

THE FRANÇAISE REALIZES ITS MISTAKE

Bernhardt's critics predicted that her rashness would cost her her career—that without the backing of France's most prestigious theater she would soon disappear from the stage. But Bernhardt had other ideas. The competition for audiences in London at the time was fierce. The tremendously popular English stars Henry Irving and Ellen Terry were playing in *The Merchant of Venice* at the Lyceum, which was adjacent to the Gaiety. The famous operatic diva Patti was singing at Covent Garden, and Gilbert and Sullivan's new light opera *The Pirates of Penzance* was delighting audiences at the Opéra Comique. Bernhardt signed a contract with the management of the Gaiety Theatre for an intermediate season.

She took full advantage of the Gaiety's offer to choose her own actors and select her own plays. The Gaiety gave her the

I n Copenhagen, Bernhardt realized she had achieved international fame. Crowds lined the streets to cheer her as she passed. On opening night, the Royal Theater was filled with royalty: the king and queen of Denmark, the king and queen of the Hellenes, and the Princess of Wales. When the play ended, the two queens tossed their bouquets onto the stage. The leading actor presented the bouquets to Bernhardt, who clutched them to her heart amid a thunderous ovation. While in Denmark, Bernhardt sailed on the king's yacht to Elsinore, where she viewed Hamlet's tomb and drank from Ophelia's well. (Later, Bernhardt would create a striking bas-relief sculpture of Ophelia wearing a garland of flowers; she would also later play the title role in *Hamlet*.) Before she left the country, the king of Denmark presented her with the diamond-studded Order of Merit.

freedom to choose roles that showcased her talents as an actress and plays with popular appeal, and her unerring instinct for good theater made her an instant success as actress-manager. One of her successful choices was *Froufrou,* whose frivolous heroine enters an unfortunate marriage, leaves her husband because of a misunderstanding, returns to beg his forgiveness, and finally dies before his eyes after he has fought a duel with her lover. The emotional role seemed made for Bernhardt, who would make it a mainstay in her repertoire.

London audiences filled the Gaiety for every performance, and the British press praised her acting lavishly. Even Parisian critics who crossed the Channel, perhaps hoping to see her downfall, were forced to admit that she was succeeding beyond all expectations. When she returned to Paris, a delegation from the Comédie Française called to beg her to return to the theater. After enjoying the freedom to chose her own roles and her own company, Bernhardt had no intention of returning to the tradition-bound theater where she was cramped by rules and regulations at every turn. Besides, she had discovered that she could make much more money as an independent actress. She thanked the members of the delegation, embraced them, showed them her impressive box office receipts from London, and set about conquering audiences in Brussels and Copenhagen. After that, she would be ready for her next big adventure: the New World.

The First American Tour

1880–1883

Permanent success cannot be achieved except by incessant intellectual labour, always inspired by the ideal.

—Sarah Bernhardt, *The Art of the Theatre* (1924)

As soon as Edward Jarrett had read of Bernhardt's break with the Comédie Française, he hurried across the English Channel with a contract for an extensive tour of North America. It provided that she select the eight plays to be performed and the actors to make up the company. Bernhardt had told Jarrett outright that she would *never* tour in the New World, but the financial arrangements were irresistible, for she was still in debt for her house and still spending twice as much as she was earning.

The terms of her contract are stunning. In 1880, when the dollar had real buying power, she was to receive $1,000 per

An American caricature. Although she was hesitant at first to tour in America, Bernhardt's American debut was a resounding success. Plays were chosen for the tour that allowed the actress to express her depth of talent most effectively, and American audiences delighted in the charm, energy, and passion she conveyed as well as the attitudes she had come to represent through the stories of her adventures. Still, by this time her excesses and her exoticism had inspired caricatures such as this one, which satirizes the immense wealth that her audiences showered on her.

performance, plus 50 percent of the gross if the receipts exceeded $4,000 a night. She would receive additional hotel expenses and would travel in a special train with her own private car. Salaries would be paid for two maids, two cooks, a waiter, and Madame Guérard.

The contract stipulated that Bernhardt would furnish her own wardrobe for the roles she would play. As she had expensive taste and was very particular about her professional costumes, this meant a huge outlay. She studied books and paintings on period dress and designed her theatrical wardrobe down to the last detail with complete disregard for costs. Her silks were woven in Lyon, her velvets were imported from Italy, and her sables and chinchilla furs from Russia. Beads of rare crystal, inserts of mother-of-pearl, and tiny, hand-stitched satin tea roses adorned her costumes. She paid 10,000 francs for the ball gown that she would wear as Marguérite in *La Dame aux Camélias*—the equivalent of about $25,000 in current terms. She wore as many as half a dozen costumes in any given play, so the money she invested in wardrobe was staggering.

She chose the plays for her American debut carefully. Each of them would showcase her special talents—especially in the dying scenes. They included *Phèdre, Hernani,* and *Froufrou,* as well as *Adrienne Lecouvreur,* whose heroine dies dramatically from poison. Also in the repertoire was *La Dame aux Camélias* by Alexandre Dumas *fils*—a new play for her, and one that would prove to be enormously popular.

Recruiting members for the acting troupe proved to be difficult. The French were well known for their reluctance to travel abroad. Most of them knew America chiefly from James Fenimore Cooper's novels, and although they found his descriptions of adventures in the New World exciting, they were not eager to experience them first hand. Her leading man was Edouard Angelo, an unexceptional actor, but a strong, handsome man who had been one of her lovers for several years. She asked her sister Jeanne to be a member of the group. Since the deaths of Judith and Régina, Bernhardt and her remaining half sister had grown closer, but Jeanne had become a morphine addict, and just before the departure date, she took an overdose of drugs, winding up in a sanatorium. To replace Jeanne, Bernhardt asked Marie Colombier to join the troupe at the last minute. The two women had known each other since girlhood, when they had been struggling to make names for themselves in their chosen profession. Now Sarah was a shining star, and Marie was a disappointed actress. She agreed to go, but it would prove to be an unhappy choice for Bernhardt.

NEW YORK APPEARANCE

Thanks to Jarrett, the French troupe's arrival in New York was greeted by boatloads of newspaper reporters and celebrity seekers. For months, the energetic agent had fed the news sources sensational accounts of his star's triumphs in Europe and her eccentric private life. Bernhardt listened to the welcoming speeches, accepted armloads of flowers, and

Following Bernhardt's first series of performances in New York City, Jarrett introduced her to Thomas Alva Edison at his home in Menlo Park, New Jersey. A pleasant supper was served, and Bernhardt (who thought Edison resembled Napoleon) charmed the bashful scientist. Captivated, Edison took her on a tour of his laboratory. She spoke with one of Edison's aides, at a distance of a mile, using an unfamiliar new device called a "telephone." Then, Edison demonstrated the phonograph, his latest invention, by singing "Yankee Doodle Dandy" off-key. She made her first recording by reciting some lines from *Phèdre*. The next day headlines in newspapers read: THE MOST FAMOUS MAN IN THE UNITED STATES MEETS THE MOST FAMOUS WOMAN IN FRANCE. (*The Divine Sarah*, 174) stood at rapt attention during the playing of *La Marseillaise*. She endured an endless line of greeters who shook her hands until her rings cut into her fingers. When she could stand it no longer, she pretended to faint and swooned gracefully into Jarrett's arms. Even he was taken in, but after the room cleared she jumped up and gleefully waltzed the agent around the room.

If Jarrett spared no effort in his blatant publicity, he was equally energetic in seeing that his precious golden goose lacked nothing in comfort. Her rooms at the fashionable Hotel Albemarle on lower Fifth Avenue were furnished in a style to make her feel at home. There were busts of Molière, Racine, and Victor Hugo on loan from an art dealer, a parlor decorated with bearskin rugs, potted palms, enormous vases of flowers, and a divan piled with satin cushions under a canopy of Persian hangings like the one in her home in Paris. Bernhardt loved it, and she loved the rush and excitement of New York. The traffic, the tall buildings, and the networked cables of the partially completed Brooklyn Bridge, all delighted her.

And she delighted New Yorkers. If the majority of those who attended her debut in *Adrienne Lecouvreur* on November 8, 1880, came out of curiosity to see a scandalous Frenchwoman, they remained to be spellbound by a distinguished French actress. The performance was a complete triumph for Bernhardt. Despite the fact that most of the audience did not understand French, her voice and her ability to project emotions through facial expressions and gestures captivated them. There was no rustling of translation leaflets when she was on stage; every eye was riveted on her. She received 27 curtain calls and numerous baskets of flowers. Back at her hotel, she stepped onto her balcony time after time, like royalty, to greet the crowd gathered in the bitter cold below. A brass band played *La Marseillaise* as she blew kisses to her cheering fans.

The critics were equally charmed by her artistry, and she received rave reviews in the *New York Times* and the New York *Herald*. Women's magazine pages were filled with pictures of her and her Paris gowns, descriptions of her Paris home, and revelations of her opinions on everything from writers to make-up. Jarrett was quick to exploit her popularity, and she endorsed perfume, candy, gloves, dresses, hair curlers, and even cigars for hefty fees.

Few actors then or now could compete with the energy displayed by this fragile-looking actress, whose extreme thinness caricaturists loved to depict. During the company's 27-day stay in New York, Bernhardt gave 27 performances in seven different plays. Her most popular role was that of Marguérite in *Las Dame aux Camélias*. Overcome by her exquisite suffering as the repentant sinner, audiences wept audibly during the death scene.

BOSTON, CANADA, AND POINTS WEST AND SOUTH

Bernhardt found Boston even more pleasing than New York. Many of the proper Bostonians she encountered during the company's two-week engagement spoke French. She especially liked the cultivated women, who welcomed her into their homes in a way the more snobbish society women of New York had not. The critics, too, showed a deeper appreciation of her as an artist while ignoring the more colorful aspects of her reputation. However, her insatiable curiosity and inability to resist a challenge led to an incident that plagued her for weeks.

Soon after her arrival in Boston, Henry Smith, the owner of a cod fishing fleet, urged Bernhardt to come to the harbor to view an enormous whale his crew had captured. The whale, with two harpoons in its sides, was moored to a dock in the Charles River. Always eager for new experiences, Bernhardt agreed to be taken to the dock to view the whale on exhibit. The next morning in a freezing rain, she was driven to the dock followed by a parade of carriages. As she stood on the quay, intrigued, Henry Smith grabbed her hand and led her down a flight of slippery steps onto the back of the whale. After spending a few minutes of slipping and sliding on the whale's back, he insisted that she pull out one of the whale's small loose bones. Reluctantly, she did so and retreated back to her carriage.

To her horror, the next day every Boston paper carried a sketch of her ripping a huge bone from the whale's back. Worse, a horse-drawn billboard bearing a color picture of the event and accompanied by a calliope toured the streets urging people to "Come and See the Enormous Cetacean that Sarah Bernhardt Killed Ripping from it Whalebones for her Corsets." (*My Double Life*, 271) In vain, she protested that she never wore corsets. The disgusting billboard and band followed her to New Haven, Hartford, and Springfield.

When Bernhardt announced she would return to Europe immediately, Jarrett showed her their contract and reminded her of the fortune still to be made on the tour. Oblivious to her distress, Henry Smith greeted her in the lobby of her hotel in New Haven and received several resounding slaps on his beaming face. At each stop, Smith sent her immense bouquets of flowers that she immediately stomped to pieces. When she was taken to visit the Remington firearms factory in Springfield, she fired one of their cannons and bought a pistol for protection when they traveled west—perhaps with the wishful thought of shooting Henry Smith. Only when the troupe crossed the Canadian border did she escape the dreaded whale publicity.

Publicity of another, more helpful kind awaited her in Montreal, where the Catholic archbishop had preached for weeks on the immorality of French plays and forbidden his congregations to see the sinful woman who performed in them. The result, of course, was that people flocked to every performance. French-Canadian students were especially

Bernhardt as Marguérite, circa 1913. In what was often considered her most famous role—Marguérite in *La Dame aux Camélias*—Bernhardt portrayed a repentant sinner, a kind of courtesan who is redeemed through love and sacrifice. Her sense of suffering was so eloquent that audiences were often overcome with emotion. Their enthusiasm for the actress who could evoke such feeling with her pure, bell-like voice only increased over the years.

enthusiastic, hurling bouquets toward the stage and releasing white doves with love notes and sonnets attached to their necks.

Jeanne, Sarah's half sister, had recovered from her drug-induced illness and crossed the ocean to catch up with the troupe. In Montreal, she and Sarah delighted in taking sleigh rides and playing in the snow. One afternoon they frightened

Jarrett by jumping from their sleigh and running to the St. Lawrence River to leap from ice floe to ice floe. The frantic impresario stood on the shore yelling at them to return. When they finally did, he scolded Bernhardt for risking her life and endangering the success of the tour, reminding her that if she killed herself, she would breach her contract.

The company's two-week stand in Chicago was highly successful, thanks partly to advance publicity provided by the Episcopal bishop, who denounced them eloquently before their arrival. Bernhardt felt she had discovered the "real" America in this windy city of tall buildings, roaring overhead trains, massive banks, and rushing businessmen. Her suite in the Palmer Hotel, which was furnished like an Egyptian pharaoh's dwelling, amused her, and she was amazed to find that the hotel contained several shops and restaurants. Even though she was almost a vegetarian, she insisted on visiting the stockyards, which thoroughly disgusted her with their sights, smells, and sounds.

From Chicago, the show moved on. Bernhardt sat in her rocking chair on the train's platform watching America's beautiful landscape unfold. It was a brutal trip with many one-night stands, as the train puffed to New Orleans, Mobile, Atlanta, Memphis, Cincinnati, Detroit, and Pittsburgh, across the frontier to Toronto, then on to Washington, D.C., Baltimore, and Philadelphia, and finally to New York.

By that time, Bernhardt's name was a household word across America. The troupe gave a series of farewell performances in New York, ending with *The Lady of the Camellias* on May 3, 1881. Amid cries of "Come back, Sarah, come back!" (Gold, 187), she took 14 curtain calls and received more than a hundred bouquets and several gifts of jewelry. Two days later, the company boarded the *America*, bound for home. The tour had been a huge financial success; Bernhardt had earned roughly the equivalent of what today would be a million dollars.

MARRIAGE

Despite her undeniable success in North America, Bernhardt's detractors in Paris continued to believe that she had been a failure and that her star was on the decline. Marie Colombier was largely responsible for this opinion. When Jeanne had joined the troupe in the United States, Bernhardt had rather callously turned Colombier's best roles over to her half sister. Because Colombier had joined the troupe as a favor to Bernhardt at the last moment, she didn't have a contract and she was naturally unhappy. She sent a series of spiteful newspaper articles back to France in which she elaborated on the mishaps of the trip and made no mention of its successes. Although much of what she wrote was untrue or greatly exaggerated, it was amusing, and it was believed.

After a few restless weeks in Paris, waiting in vain for offers to act, Bernhardt crossed the English Channel for her third season on the London stage. Again she was highly successful in that country, which was always more tolerant of her behavior than her homeland. Members of British society, including the Prince of Wales, found her charming and went out of their way to welcome and entertain her. Young people made a cult out of Sarah Bernhardt worship and kept scrapbooks filled with pictures and newspaper articles about her. British actors appreciated her professional ability. The great English actress Ellen Terry became a close friend and called her "Sally B."

Following the London engagement, Bernhardt and her company embarked on a grand European tour. In Italy, Greece, Switzerland, Belgium, and Holland, crowned heads invited her to give command performances and presented her with precious jewelry. The public flocked to see her act and lined the streets to catch glimpses of her as she passed by in her carriage. In Russia, the tsar insisted on bowing to her rather than letting her curtsy to him.

Somewhere along the way—just how and where is

Aristidis ("Jacques") Damala. Sarah Bernhardt met, fell in love with, and married Aristidis Damala. Damala was a young, wealthy, handsome Greek man, considered arrogant enough for Bernhardt's friends to wonder why she found him attractive. Through the years, the relationship would prove very draining for Bernhardt, both emotionally and financially, as Damala's habits leaned more and more toward gambling, drugs, and affairs. Because she was Catholic, Bernhardt did not consider divorce, though eventually she did obtain a legal separation from him. Still, he called on her in times of need, and she continued to offer support and assistance until the time of his death.

unclear—she met a handsome young Greek man named Aristidis Damala, called Jacques, and fell passionately in love with him. His father had made a fortune in the Greek shipping business, and moved the family to France. After finishing his education, Damala returned to his homeland, where he became a dashing cavalry officer in the Greek army. He also became a gambler, a womanizer, and a drug addict. He prided himself on conquering any woman he met. Certainly Bernhardt was not lacking in ardent suitors. Her leading men, including Angelo, often wanted to marry her, and almost every mail brought proposals. Her friends were baffled by her attraction to this arrogant man who was eleven years her junior. Never one to listen to advice and warnings, Bernhardt ignored all reports of his bad behavior and determined to make him her own.

Dismissing the leading man on the tour, she put Damala in his place. Although she coached him in his roles, he was never more than a mediocre actor. But audiences, aware of the Bernhardt–Damala affair, flocked to the theaters to see them perform love scenes together. Bernhardt was as blind to his defects as an actor as she was to his defects as a man. She proposed marriage, and he accepted. He had run through his family inheritance; his debts were piling up; and his drug habit was increasingly expensive.

Since Bernhardt was a Roman Catholic and Damala was Greek Orthodox, they could not obtain a marriage license in France. *Quand même*, they eloped to England and were married in St. Andrew's Church on April 4, 1882. Probably the only person whose opinion she cared about was that of her son, Maurice, who greeted the news with bitterness and open hostility.

Bernhardt stubbornly continued to cast Damala as her leading man. In plays such as *La Dame*, she received rave reviews as usual, but although some critics softened their reviews of Damala's acting for her sake, few of them could find many

"Bernhardt on the war path." Returning to France following a successful American tour, Bernhardt discovered that her success in North America had been misrepresented to the French press. Marie Colombier, a disgruntled actress from the tour who had lost many of her best roles to Bernhardt's sister, is credited with having encouraged rumors of failure and disgrace. Colombier later published a scandalous biography of her former friend, *The Memoirs of Sarah Barnum* (see sidebar, chapter 7). As this illustration of Bernhardt and Colombier printed in *The Police Gazette* suggests, Bernhardt's reaction was severe—she and her son attacked Colombier with stage weapons and drove her from her house.

positive things to say about his performances. With his distorted ego, Damala blamed Bernhardt for the criticism he received.

In autumn of 1882, Bernhardt began to collaborate with a playwright who would open a new phase and add more luster to her already illustrious career. Victorien Sardou offered his play *Fédora* to Bernhardt, but absolutely refused to allow Damala to play the leading man. Desperate to please the two most important men in her life, Bernhardt purchased the Ambigu Theatre in Paris, making Maurice the manager and scheduling a lavish and expensive production starring Damala there. When this production proved to be unpopular, and Bernhardt's own appearance in *Fédora* was a smashing success, Damala was enraged.

Their home—or rather, Bernhardt's home, where they lived—became the scene of loud, ugly quarrels. She protested furiously when she realized that some of the debts she was paying for him were for gifts for other women. He argued that she had snared him into marriage and that he had a right to enjoy himself. He accused her of stifling his acting career. Calling her every bad name he could think of, he stormed out of the house. The next day she learned he had left for North Africa to enlist in the army there. Despite her success in *Fédora*, Bernhardt was hurt and depressed over her failed marriage, although she never quit working. Considering her spending habits and those of her spoiled son, she could not afford to.

Actress and Manager

1884–1893

Alas, we are the victims of advertisement. Those who taste the joys and sorrows of fame when they have passed forty, know how to look after themselves. They know what is concealed beneath the flowers, and what the gossip, the calumnies, and the praise are worth. But as for those who win fame when they are twenty, they know nothing, and are caught up in the whirlpool.

—Sarah Bernhardt, *The Art of the Theatre* (1924)

I have often been asked why I am so fond of playing male parts. . . . As a matter of fact, it is not male parts, but male brains that I prefer.

—Sarah Bernhardt, *The Art of the Theatre* (1924)

THE END OF BERNHARDT'S MARRIAGE
Thanks to Damala's desertion and the youthful Maurice's mismanagement, the Ambigu Theatre, into which Bernhardt

Bernhardt as Théodora. Victorien Sardou created the spectacular *Théodora* as a vehicle for Bernhardt's talents, and the collaboration was a total success. Bernhardt was always extremely fastidious about her costumes, so she and Sardou traveled to Ravenna to research the empress from mosaics at the Church of San Vitale. Costumes like this one were hard for Bernhardt to move in, but she found a way—and the audiences at *Théodora* were almost as impressed by the extravagance of the scenery and costumes as by the drama itself. Bernhardt often spent thousands of francs on her costumes; this one was liberally studded with semiprecious stones.

had sunk a small fortune, was in trouble. By February of 1883, Bernhardt was forced to sell her jewelry and her carriages at auction to keep from losing her house to creditors. To raise more money, she arranged a lucrative tour of Scandinavia. Accompanying her was the poet and playwright Jean Richepin, whose loving attention soothed her anguish over her unhappy marriage. Richepin was the opposite of Damala—manly, cheerful, full of energy, and completely devoted to Bernhardt.

The tour was a huge success, with audiences and critics praising her performances, particularly the final act of *Fédora* in which she expired in her lover's arms after taking poison. Returning home to find Damala calmly lying in her bed reading, she took him back. He was hopelessly addicted to morphine, which was easily obtained at that time. He no longer bothered to hide his habit. Bernhardt, desperate to curb it, broke her umbrella over the head of the druggist who was supplying him—with no effect except for the loss of her umbrella. Damala disrupted her play rehearsals, criticized everything she did, and openly carried on an affair with a younger actress in her company. When he went to Monte Carlo with the girl and lost heavily at the gambling tables, he wired Bernhardt for help. She scraped up the money and sent it to him. Their quarrels were gleefully reported in the scandal sheets, and Bernhardt suffered constant humiliation. When she finally threw away all the morphine and syringes she could find, Damala left again, and she obtained a legal separation. As a Roman Catholic, she did not consider divorce.

Hoping to increase her income, Bernhardt leased the Porte Saint-Martin Theater in Paris. As actress-manager, she produced and performed in *Froufrou* and *La Dame*, making good profits. Then she made the mistake of putting on a play Richepin wrote for her; it was a disaster. To make matters worse, Damala, who had again taken the "cure" at a clinic, was appearing with some success at another local theater in a play called *The Master Blacksmith*. One afternoon he appeared at a matinee of Bernhardt's play in which she and Richepin were performing in front of a half-empty house to an audience that was falling asleep. Every time his ex-wife approached the footlights, Damala would shake his head and sigh, "Poor Sarah." When the play ended, Richepin rushed to the main exit and beat Damala severely.

Bernhardt and Richepin collaborated on several more plays, none of which was received with any enthusiasm. Then Victorien Sardou came to the rescue with a new play he had written as a showcase for her talents. *Théodora* is about the empress who, with Emperor Justinian, ruled sixth-century Byzantium. In actual life, Théodora was a woman of humble birth—her father was the bear keeper at the Constantinople circus—who became an actress while quite young. She led the life of a courtesan, giving birth to at least one illegitimate child. Attracted by her beauty and intelligence, Justinian married her in A.D. 525. Sardou's play is a melodrama in which Théodora kills a would-be assassin by stabbing him with a long, ornamental gold hairpin. In the last scene, she is led offstage with a rope around her neck to be put to death for being unfaithful to the emperor.

Audiences came to see the elaborate Byzantium stage sets and fabulous costumes as much as they did to see the performance. Both Sardou and Bernhardt had visited the Church of San Vitale in Ravenna, Italy, where they studied the impressive mosaic portraits of Théodora and Justinian. Bernhardt made detailed sketches of the empress's robes and jewelry so Parisian dress designers and jewelers could copy them. Her ability to move around so gracefully under the weight of the heavy crown and costumes encrusted with thousands of semiprecious stones was a marvel in itself. The oriental splendor of the sets with their massive pillars, soaring arches, mosaics, furniture set with silver and precious stones, and backdrops displaying lavish gardens and the city's golden domes dazzled the onlookers. *Théodora* was a smashing success both in Paris, where it ran for 300 performances, and in London, where it ran for more than 100.

SOUTH AMERICAN TOUR

In the spring of 1886, Edward Jarrett arranged a South American tour for Bernhardt, who embarked at Bordeaux with Maurice, a large troupe of actors and assistants, several animals, 40 cases of theatrical costumes, and more than 80 trunks in tow. The trip was one long triumph. In Rio de Janeiro, Dom Pedro II, the emperor of Brazil, attended every performance of her plays and presented her with a gold bracelet.

I n December of 1883, a vulgar little book, *The Memoirs of Sarah Barnum* by Marie Colombier, appeared in Paris bookstores. Using thinly disguised fictional characters, Colombier expressed her resentment of Bernhardt by depicting her, her mother, her son, and other relatives and friends as depraved. When the book was brought to her attention, Bernhardt, with Richepin at her side, stormed into Colombier's apartment. At the sight of Bernhardt with a riding whip in one hand and a dagger in the other, and Richepin armed with a large carving knife, Colombier wisely fled through a concealed door. Bernhardt rushed through the rooms slashing fabrics and shattering china, glass, and porcelain objects, and she left the apartment in shambles.

News of the attack received much media attention, and it was lampooned in numerous cartoons in France and other European countries. *Sarah Barnum*, which had been largely ignored by the public, became a red-hot best-seller. New York newspapers played up "The Bernhardt Attack." One critic opined, "Certainly Sarah Bernhardt would have done better to stay at home for the sake of her dignity as an artist, and allow public disdain to take care of the abominable book." (*The Divine Sarah*, 209)

Then, en route from Rio to Montevideo, Uruguay, Jarrett suffered a heart attack and died. Bernhardt experienced terrible shock, but remained committed to the tour with Maurice Grau, Jarrett's New York partner, taking over as manager.

In Buenos Aires, elegantly dressed men stood at the stage door and spread their handkerchiefs on the ground for her to walk on. Bernhardt's 20 performances in that city brought 80,000 Argentineans to ogle her. Before the dangerous passage around the tip of South America, she sent Maurice back to France. She missed her self-centered son and wrote him long letters, asking him to send her his photograph and a "little" telegram on her birthday.

The troupe traveled up the west coast of South America, stopping to perform in Valparaiso and Santiago, Chile, and briefly in Lima, Peru. Hotel accommodations and traveling conditions grew increasingly primitive; large cockroaches crawled up the legs of tables as they ate and mosquitoes made sleep difficult. Even so, Bernhardt proved to be an intrepid traveler, thriving on new adventures in her free time. She went big game hunting several times, and in Ecuador, she went on a crocodile hunt. In Panama, her two leading men came down with mild cases of yellow fever, and she was saddened when her maid died of it.

After successful performances in Mexico, the troupe entered the United States through Texas. From there they toured the eastern states, performing in large cities and small towns as Bernhardt had done on her first American tour seven years earlier. In April, they reached New York. On the voyage home, Bernhardt suffered a bad fall that seriously injured her right knee; this knee would pain her for the next 20 years.

Bernhardt returned to France after 13 months of strenuous traveling and performing with a nice profit, some stuffed crocodile hides, the head of a large antelope she claimed to have shot, and a live tigress she had acquired. Scarcely taking time to catch her breath, she returned to London in May. From there, she toured England, Ireland, and Scotland. After a successful summer in the British Isles, she again returned to France, having earned a huge sum of money from her many long months of work.

She immediately set about spending her profits, buying a house at 56 Boulevard Pereire, which would be her home for the rest of her life. Over the main entrance, the initials "S.B." were carved. *Quand même* appeared over the fireplace, on her linens, and in gold on her fine china. The house was furnished with a clutter that was startling even to Victorian sentiment. Everywhere she had traveled she had collected: primitive masks, South American daggers, silver objects from Mexico, gilded mirrors from Venice, statuary from Greece, tapestries, and animal skin rugs with snarling heads. Her famous divan dominated the main salon, which was filled with a profusion of flowers and rare, costly plants, in addition to busts and paintings, some by Bernhardt herself, of her, Maurice, and the family dogs. Her love of animals was evident in the large bowl of fat goldfish, the yapping dogs, the twittering birds, and occasional wild animals. Bernhardt reigned as queen of her new domain, and her "court," consisting of family, friends, professional associates, and supporters, enjoyed the lavish entertainments she provided.

LA TOSCA

On November 24, 1887, Bernhardt appeared in *La Tosca*, a new play Sardou had created for her. She had refused to allow the French press to attend the dress rehearsal, and her ongoing feud with them continued. One of the chief French critics condemned Sardou for writing a play that was clearly intended for export, as it was fit only for "ignorant Englishmen and American savages."(Aston, 66) The British and Americans did indeed celebrate Bernhardt's portrayal of Floria Tosca, as did most everyone in Paris, the newspaper critics excepted.

Set in Rome in 1800, the play combines political intrigue with passionate desire and jealousy. The fourth act contains the

Bernhardt in Sardou's *La Tosca*, 1887. Victorien Sardou created the role of Floria Tosca, a singer who murders for love, as another vehicle for Bernhardt; the actress originated the role in 1887, between an extended tour of North and South America and a year-long European tour, and she performed in *La Tosca* for the next 25 years. Like the roles of Phaedra and Marguérite, the role of Tosca would become a signature for Bernhardt; its intensity fit her style of performance with astounding results. Years later, the play was later developed into an opera by the celebrated composer Giacomo Puccini.

famous scene in which Tosca stabs the villain Scarpia to death and, in accordance with her Catholic faith, administers last rites to him. In the final act, she learns that her lover is dead and leaps to her death from the battlements of St. Angelo prison. On July 10, 1888, the London *Pall Mall Gazette* reported: "A more exhausting part has never fallen to the lot of any actress; but the effect is correspondingly intense." The emotion generated by the play was so intense that women in the audiences became hysterical, and sometimes men left mid-performance, overcome by powerful feelings. Bernhardt herself cried real tears at every performance and sometimes actually fainted during Tosca's fainting scene. Along with *Phèdre* and *La Dame*, *Tosca* would become a staple in her acting repertoire.

FAMILY EVENTS

On December 29, 1887, an event occurred that had profound significance for Bernhardt: the marriage of Maurice. At 23, he was a handsome man-about-town, charming when he wished to be, fond of dueling and gambling, and dependent on his mother for his livelihood. His bride was a pretty Polish princess named Terka Jablonowska. At the wedding ceremony in a fashionable Parisian church, Bernhardt nearly upstaged the bride, as every head craned to watch her float up the aisle wearing a soft pink faille dress with a cloak of gray velvet and marabou feathers framing her smiling face.

In private, Bernhardt shed many tears over the wedding. She was fond of Terka and approved of the marriage, but it was hard for her to share her son, the one true love of her life, with another woman. She wore his portrait and a lock of his hair in a gold locket around her neck, and she carried the shoes he had worn as a child with her on tour. In his own way, Maurice was equally devoted to her: Several of the duels he had fought were to defend her honor from insulting critics and cartoonists. Before the wedding, he promised to visit her every day, and he kept his word whenever she was not on tour.

Maurice Bernhardt. From the time of his birth, Sarah Bernhardt's son, Maurice, remained a significant focus of her life. On December 29, 1887, at the age of 23, Maurice married Terka Jablonowska, a Polish princess. Bernhardt found it difficult to share the attention of her son with another woman, but she approved of the marriage and continued to support her son in all aspects of his life. Maurice became accustomed to his mother's support, relying on her for his livelihood and the repayment of his significant gambling debts. He also, in many ways, did return the devotion shown to him by his mother, keeping his promise to visit her every day when she was not on tour.

Despite Maurice's frequent visits to her home and his pre-performance visits to her dressing room, Bernhardt missed living with her son. To fill the void in her life, she devoted herself to her work. In the spring of 1888, she embarked on a 12-month tour of Europe, giving performances in Italy, Egypt, Turkey, Sweden, Norway, and Russia. *Tosca* was an enormous hit with audiences and critics everywhere.

Returning to Paris in March of 1889, Bernhardt received news that Damala had become ill. He begged her to visit him. He had not worked since his brief success in *The Master Blacksmith*, and he sank ever deeper into his drug addition. Bernhardt rushed to his bedside and found him in a dingy room with grains of cocaine and morphine littering the filthy floor. The only ornaments in the dismal room were a saber and gold crown, both from plays in which he had appeared, and a battered Greek flag.

Bernhardt took Damala to her home and arranged for the best medical attention available. He rallied briefly, but he never recovered from his drug-induced illness. In a touching gesture, Bernhardt asked him to appear with her in *La Dame aux Camélias*. He eagerly accepted, although they both knew he was in no condition to perform. The revival of *La Dame* ran for six weeks—with Bernhardt receiving rave reviews and the critics asking what was wrong with the leading man. Damala had lost his strength to morphine, as well as his looks and his voice. When he went into a complete physical collapse, he was taken to a hospital, where he died on August 18, 1889, at the age of 34.

Bernhardt sent Damala's body back to Greece along with a bust of him to adorn his tomb. She did not forget the husband who had caused her so much grief. In later years, whenever tours took her to Athens, she called on his mother and visited his grave to cover it with flowers. She wore mourning for several months after his death and signed legal documents "Sarah Bernhardt Damala, widow." At 45, Bernhardt was a widow and a grandmother. Terka had just given birth to Simone, the first of two daughters.

JOAN OF ARC AND CLEOPATRA

From time to time, letters from parents appeared in Paris news-papers asking Bernhardt to appear as a "pure" heroine in a moral play so they could take their daughters to see the distinguished actress. In January of 1890, she satisfied their request by appear-ing as the saintly Joan of Arc. Adapted from the libretto for an opera with splendid music by Gounod, Barbier's *Jeanne d'Arc* was a grand spectacle, with sets constructed to resemble the old market square and the inside of the cathedral in Rheims.

On opening night, when the 45-year-old grandmother as the Maid of Orleans was asked by her inquisitors to state her age, she slowly turned to face the audience and proudly answered: "Nineteen!" The declaration brought down the house; and almost 20 years later, when as a 65-year-old great-grandmother she played the same scene, the audience was even more enthusiastic. Even the most skeptical critics fell under the spell of her Joan, and the famous novelist Anatole France wrote: "She is poetry itself. . . . She is legend come to life." (Gold, 244)

The role called for her to fall to her knees repeatedly, which caused her a great deal of pain. After 16 weeks of torture, her right knee became so dangerously inflamed her doctor ordered two months of bed rest, and she was forced to close the play. By June, however, she was sufficiently recovered to take *Jeanne d'Arc* to London for a successful summer season.

Bernhardt's period of sainthood did not last long. In October, she returned to Sardou and sin as the seductress Cleopatra. It was definitely not a production to please the parents of young girls. It was a role that gave her the opportunity to wear ornate, exotic costumes and a chance for tempestuous action. For the death scene, in which the distraught queen is bitten by an asp, Bernhardt kept two garter snakes in a jewel case on her dressing table. She was fond of them and often twined them around her wrists, to the horror of her maid and visitors. In the scene in which a slave brings news of Antony's marriage, Cleopatra stabs the messenger and turns her anger on the palace, smashing goblets and tearing

Poster for *Jeanne d'Arc* at the Théâtre de la Renaissance.
When she performed the role of Joan of Arc, young girls at
last had the opportunity to see the great Sarah Bernhardt,
as other characters portrayed by the actress were considered
inappropriate for such an impressionable audience. Bernhardt
performed the role of the pure-hearted 19-year-old
heroine while she herself was 45 and 65 years of age,
though the conviction of her performance made believers
of even the most skeptical viewers. Her famous "*dix-neuf
ans*" drew enthusiastic applause whenever she performed
this role. This poster was created by Eugène Samuel Grasset
(1841–1917), whose work was at the center of the Art
Nouveau movement in Paris and influenced such artists
as Alphonse Mucha, Paul Berthon, William Bradley, and
Maxfield Parrish.

down draperies in a jealous rage. One critic attributed Bernhardt's power to spellbind an audience partly to her voice: "She could express anything, from the fury of the whirlwind to the sigh of a sleepy stream." And the great Anatole France could only cry, "What charm, what magic!" (Richardson, 131)

WORLD AMBASSADOR

In 1891, it was announced that Madame Sarah Bernhardt was to embark on a Grand World Tour that would last almost three years. The news was carried in papers worldwide, and elaborate preparations were made for receptions in the cities where she would be performing. Her tour was like a royal progress with reporters referring to her as "The greatest of French ambassadors." She played the role of ambassador to perfection, responding to cries of "*Vive la France*," by holding out her arms and crying in her vibrant voice "*Vive*" whatever country she was in with a simple sincerity that won the hearts of the natives. (Skinner, 248-249)

She probably listened to more renditions of *La Marseillaise* and attended more official receptions than she cared to, but she took the obligation to represent her country seriously. She also took her work seriously, directing as well as acting in the 15 plays in the company's repertoire, calling for endless rehearsals and attending to every detail, including checking box office receipts.

In Australia, where she was considered the greatest actress in the world, she played in Melbourne and Adelaide, as well as Sydney. Everywhere she was greeted with red carpets, booming cannons, and huge crowds, and adoring Australian fans presented her with a koala bear and a wallaby.

From Auckland, Honolulu, and Samoa, across the length and breadth of the United States from San Francisco to Brooklyn, from Buffalo to Galveston, through South America, and across the whole of Europe from Russia to Lisbon, she and her troupe traveled. On September 29, 1893, Bernhardt returned home triumphant and richer by some 3.5 million francs.

8

Curtain Calls

1894–1923

> We must live for the few who know and appreciate us, who judge and absolve us, and for whom we have the same affection and indulgence. The rest I look upon as a mere crowd, lively or sad, loyal or corrupt, from whom there is nothing to be expected but fleeting emotions, either pleasant or unpleasant, which leave no trace behind them.
> —Sarah Bernhardt, quoted in *The Memoirs of Sarah Bernhardt*

BELLE ISLE

After her strenuous travels, even the indefatigable Sarah Bernhardt needed a rest, and she'd found the ideal spot. Before the Grand World Tour, she had purchased an old coast guard fort on the tip of a tiny island in Brittany that the French called *Belle Île en Mer* ("Beautiful Island in the Sea"). The wild landscape, the somber beauty of the rugged cliffs, and the spectacular view of the vast ocean delighted

Sarah Bernhardt at her dressing table, one month before her death. Bernhardt continued to work in whatever capacity she could until the time of her death. She died in the arms of her son, Maurice, on March 26, 1923; she was laid to rest in the legendary coffin that her mother had bought for her many years before, when doctors had led her to expect an early death. This photograph is the last ever taken of "the Divine Sarah."

her, and she set about making a paradise for herself, family, and friends.

With her usual enthusiasm and disregard for costs, she plunged into planning her island retreat. A park was laid out and steps cut into the rocks leading down to the sea. Partitions in the old fort were knocked down to create comfortable

Belle Île. Bernhardt spent the last years of her life in the comfort of the island retreat she had built for herself, her friends, and her family on Belle Île. Sparing no expense—as had become her custom—Bernhardt spent nearly 4 million francs creating this island paradise, including lavish furnishings and decorations, seaweed baths, private cottages for guests enjoying extended stays, and, of course, her famous and ever-changing entourage of exotic animals.

bedrooms. The long, vaulted hall was converted into a combined dining room, salon, and studio. Comfortable sofas surrounded the hall's immense fireplace. The narrow slits in the walls were replaced by large windows that overlooked the sea. Best of all was the sunny half-open courtyard that became known as the "Sarahtorium." Sheltered from the wind, it was furnished with cushioned wicker furniture and garden tables and planted with little tamarisk trees, whose slender drooping leaves and spiky pink flowers Bernhardt admired.

Here, after the heavy midday meal, she and her guests gathered for a quiet time. Some sketched or read while Bernhardt dozed, her face covered with veils to protect it from the sun. After her siesta, she would spring up and lead the others on a hike. At five o'clock, it was time for tennis, played by the rules of the lady of the house. Although she served well and returned balls vigorously, she refused to move an inch. If she was unable to hit the ball without moving, she became upset. Maurice learned to play her game expertly, but some of the guests, who shook at the thought of upsetting Sarah Bernhardt, preferred to hide when it was time for tennis.

Seaweed baths, which were thought to be healthful, were popular at Belle Île, and Bernhardt urged her guests to take them. For transportation, there were shaggy little ponies and a donkey cart to ride. As always, there was a changing cast of animals. In addition to the usual yapping dogs, there was a bad-tempered hawk named Alexis, after the Russian grand duke who had given it to her. Other members of the menagerie included the wildcat she had brought back from South America, monkeys, and a boa constrictor she had bought from a peón, who told her it would sleep for months as it had just eaten a whole pig. When the boa awoke suddenly and started eating the chair cushions, either she or Maurice shot it, depending on the story's teller.

In addition to hiking and tennis, Bernhardt and her guests enjoyed hunting sea birds, shrimping, and fishing. After dinner they gathered in the main salon for card games or dominos, passionate conversations, music, and dancing. Bernhardt also found time to work, studying manuscripts of plays for possible production and continuing her sculpting.

For three decades, she spent her summers at Belle Île. At first, she only went there with Maurice, Madame Guérard, and a few close friends. As the years passed, the retreat grew to resemble a little village with cottages to house family and friends. After Maurice's marriage, she built a four-room villa for him and his bride. When they had daughters, she had a second villa built for them, their nurses, and their governesses. She built a villa with a large studio for Georges Clairin and Louise Abbéma, her artist friends who spent months at Belle Île. She also had a six-room villa built for miscellaneous guests who decided to prolong their stay.

In the summer of 1906, she arrived at Belle Île to find someone building a 20-room hotel near her property. Horrified that the hotel would end her privacy, she bought the structure at an outrageous price and converted it into a house where she and all her family and guests could live under one roof. In addition, she bought all the acres in the area that were available. All in all, she spent over 4 million francs on her island retreat.

THE SARAH BERNHARDT THEATER

Bernhardt took over the management of the Renaissance Theatre in 1893 and continued to run it for five years. She was the sole producer and director, working incredibly long hours. She had workrooms installed for creating elaborate scenery and costumes, which she oversaw in every detail. She revived classical favorites, introduced 12 new plays and several new actors, rehearsed with the casts, and appeared in seven or eight performances a week. She continued to go to London for a summer season each year, and in 1896, she did a brief American tour.

In January of 1899, Bernhardt took over the Nations Theatre and renamed it the Théâtre Sarah-Bernhardt, or the Sarah Bernhardt Theatre. She managed it until her death. After the cramped space at the Renaissance Theatre, it was a joy for the actors to have a large stage, an auditorium with 1,700 seats (as opposed to the 900 at the Renaissance), room to store large pieces of scenery, and adequate dressing areas. In renovating the old building, Bernhardt created a luxurious apartment for herself that included a salon where she could receive company, a large dressing room and bath, and a dining room where she could give dinner parties between matinee and evening performances.

As always, her performances in ever-popular favorites such as *La Dame*, *Tosca*, and *Phèdre* were huge successes. Her Paris fans were charmed by her bold innovations, such as choosing to play the title role in *Hamlet*. When she was audacious enough to take the Shakespearean play to London, the British marveled at idea of a 54-year-old Frenchwoman playing the prince of Denmark. Strict traditionalists couldn't get over the idea of a woman daring to play Hamlet, but a surprising number of theater experts praised her interpretation. Even the good, gray *Times* said: "Her Hamlet is a rendering worked out with care and intelligence. . . . No one who is an admirer of Madame Bernhardt's wonderful art and wonderful personality will come away disappointed."

An equally daring experiment was her performance in *L'Aiglon* (*The Eaglet*) as Napoleon Bonaparte's only son, the frail Duc de Reichstadt who had pathetic dreams of reestablishing the Bonaparte empire. Bernhardt's interpretation of the six-act verse play by the poet-playwright Edmond Rostand was a glorious success in France. The play and Bernhardt's performance stirred the national pride in Napoleon's reign. Audiences wept and showered the stage with violets, the emblem of Napoleon. Thousands bought picture postcards of Bernhardt dressed in the trim white uniform she wore in the role of the Eaglet. Bernhardt and Rostand became devoted friends, and when he fell ill with pneumonia, she drove to his country home daily to take him "Napoleon" violets.

THE DIVINE SARAH

Performances at the Sarah Bernhardt Theatre continued to draw crowds in Paris, but it was the frequent tours of foreign countries that brought in the golden coins that Bernhardt required to support her lavish lifestyle—and to support Maurice and his gambling debts. As the years passed, the number of her fans all over the world grew. She enjoyed the great ballyhoo that occurred with her arrival in foreign countries, except for the times when she was literally mobbed and frenzied admirers snatched pins out of her hair or tore bits from her voluminous veiling. In 1905–1906, her new agents, the Shubert brothers, announced "The Farewell American Tour of Bernhardt." (There would be three more "Farewell American Tours.")

At this time, a theatrical syndicate had a tight grip on all stage productions in the United States. They decreed that "The Bernhardt" could only perform in theaters under their control, when and where they chose. The Shubert brothers flatly refused, and said they would make their own arrangements for "the divine Sarah." They did. In Atlanta, Augusta, Savannah, Tampa, and Jacksonville, the Bernhardt company played in skating rinks. In Texas, the syndicate managed to close the skating rinks to the touring company, so they performed *Camille* in a saloon in San Antonio and played in various other cities under a huge portable tent. In San Francisco, which was still smoldering from the Great Fire following the earthquake of 1906, they crossed the bay to play in the open air Greek Theater at Berkeley.

In 1908–1909, Bernhardt did a last Grand Tour of Europe with great success. Two more Farewell American Tours followed in 1910 and 1912. By that time, the syndicate had eased its stranglehold on theaters, so the French actors were able to perform on legitimate stages. Everywhere, Bernhardt was welcomed and honored by society's elite. In New York, snobbish social leaders who had closed their doors to her 25 years earlier now begged her to attend dinners and parties given for her.

In South America, a disastrous accident occurred. During a performance of *La Tosca*—in the climactic final scene in which, having murdered for her lover and then lost him to treachery, and with the police about to catch her, the heroine leaps from a castle wall—the thick mattress that should have broken Bernhardt's fall was improperly placed, and she landed on the bare boards of the stage, again injuring her troublesome right knee. She fainted from the pain, and it was two weeks before she could walk well enough to continue the tour.

Between tours, Bernhardt spent 12 to 14 hours a day at the Bernhardt Theater: teaching a class in acting, auditioning potential players, overseeing every detail of stage scenery and props, rehearsing and performing. At her Paris home, she hosted luncheons and dinners, with the "who's who" of the world as guests. A favorite guest was Theodore Roosevelt, who had been her friend for many years. They were much alike, and she said of him, "That man and I, together we could rule the world!" (Skinner, 297)

Whether she was in Paris or at Belle Île, Bernhardt's greatest pleasure was in having her granddaughters with her. After Maurice's wife, Terka, died, granddaughter Simone married and moved to London, and Lysiane came to live with her. She didn't like the term "grandmother," so the grandchildren called her "Great," which pleased her. She taught them to stay busy by creating something with their hands or minds, and each evening she asked them what they had learned during the day. As often as she could escape from her work at the theater, she took Lysiane on trips in her large Daimler limousine. She loved sharing her appreciation of the natural beauty of the world, reminding Lysiane to observe sunsets and stars, flowers and trees, and brooks and ponds.

By 1913, Bernhardt's knee was so painful that she could barely take two steps without assistance. Furniture on the stage had to be arranged so she could move from piece to piece. In her dressing room, she rubbed ether on the knee and received

December 9, 1896, was a special day in Sarah Bernhardt's life. As a tribute to the 52-year-old actress, a group of writers and actors planned a day of "glorification" to honor her for her contributions to the world of theater. At noon, 500 guests in full evening dress met in the flower-decked banquet hall of the Grand Hotel in Paris. The guests were the most famous people in their fields—science, politics, business, literature, art, society, and theater. A half-hour after they assembled, Bernhardt appeared on an overhanging balcony in a gleaming white dress embroidered in gold and trimmed with sable. As she made her dazzling entrance down the long, winding staircase, the guests rose to their feet, cheering. One reporter said: "She wafted toward us in a halo of glory." (Richardson, 151)

Bernhardt took her place at the table of honor, on a dais under a canopy of green velvet. There were three different menus for the grand dinner, designed by three different artists. The six courses included hors d'oeuvres, salmon, three choices of entrées, truffles, pâté de foie gras, salad, fruits, pastries, and, among the desserts, "Gâteau Sarah"—"Sarah Cake." Sardou proposed a toast to the guest of honor, and an

injections to deaden the pain. Still, she carried on with her work. Always interested in the latest inventions, she became involved in filmmaking. She was disappointed in the film versions of *La Tosca* and *La Dame* but thought two films, one in which she played Queen Elizabeth I and one called *Madame Sarah Bernhardt at Home*, were more successful.

As she became older and more crippled, her public continued to honor her. Every birthday was a huge celebration, and there were many "Sarah Bernhardt" days, not only in orchestra and choir performed a cantata composed for her. Another witness recorded her godlike departure:

> As she went slowly up the winding stair, from time to time sending a smile or a wave of her hand to her admirers below, she seemed almost to be mounting in triumph to the sky. (Skinner, 257)

A procession of a hundred carriages transported the celebrants to the Renaissance Theater, where Bernhardt performed the second act of *Phèdre*. Following that, the curtain rose to reveal her robed in white and gold and seated on a flower-strewn throne, with women in adoring poses surrounding her. Six of France's leading contemporary poets read sonnets they had composed in her honor. As the curtain descended, Bernhardt stood weeping as showers of camellias rained down on her. The audience was in tumult—shouting, cheering, applauding, and stamping their feet. There was no doubt in their minds, or in Bernhardt's, that they were honoring the greatest actress in the world. She had achieved the goal she had set for herself in the earliest days of her career.

France but also in other countries in which she traveled. In the spring of 1914, Sarah Bernhardt was decorated with the coveted Legion of Honour, and many friends wrote to say it was an honor long overdue for her service to her country.

QUAND MÊME

When World War I began in August 1914 and the invasion of Paris seemed likely, Bernhardt's family begged her to leave the city. She refused, saying that she would remain in Paris as she had during the war in 1870. However, when her friend Georges Clemenceau—who would become the French leader during the last years of the war—came to tell her that she was on the list of hostages the German kaiser wanted taken, she agreed to move to a villa about 25 miles from Bordeaux.

Her leg, which had become excruciatingly painful, had been in a cast for several months. When the cast was removed, it revealed that gangrene had set in and was threatening her life. Both she and the doctors knew the leg would have to be amputated above the knee. She faced the ordeal bravely, telling her stricken family and friends to "have a little courage" as she was wheeled into the operating room wearing a white satin dressing gown and swathed in gauzy pink veils.

The operation was successful, but her convalescence was long and painful. When her strength finally returned, Bernhardt tried a wooden leg but found it too cumbersome, and flying into a rage, had it thrown into the fire. She refused to use crutches or a wheelchair, which made her feel like an invalid. Instead, she had a sedan chair designed to carry her. Designed in Louis XV style, it was painted white with gilt carvings on the sides. For the rest of her life, Bernhardt appeared like a Byzantine empress in this conveyance, her mutilated figure covered in velvets and furs, her arms filled with flowers.

Her country was at war, and *quand même*, Sarah Bernhardt would do her part. She asked to join a group of theatrical people who were performing for the troops in the field. Wearing a tiger skin floor-length coat, riding in her sedan chair to and from trains, she performed bits of plays and gave patriotic speeches in mess tents, on the terraces of chateaus, in hospitals, and in barns. Her vibrant voice and final rallying cry of "To arms!" stirred the young soldiers, who rose as one and cheered themselves hoarse.

In 1916, she went to America for her final "Farewell Tour." In addition to performing short, stationary scenes, she spoke at

Bernhardt and the War. This poster, which dates to 1917, advertises a benefit performance being held at the Sarah Bernhardt Theatre for soldiers who were mutilated in World War I. Bernhardt herself became a kind of hero of the war, doing everything she could to advance the cause of the Allies. She even refused to leave Paris—for she had stayed through the turmoil of 1870—until the War Ministry convinced her that she was too great a personage to become a hostage of the Kaiser. (According to Skinner, the thought of being on a hostage list amused Bernhardt.)

Red Cross rallies, at benefits, and at other public meetings, encouraging Americans to join the Allies in the war. Lysiane accompanied her on the trip and wrote some verses that Bernhardt recited when she was named godmother to all American children at a huge ceremony in Chicago.

Bernhardt suffered from uremia and was forced to undergo a nearly fatal kidney operation in New York after eight months of strenuous touring. While she recuperated from the operation, she wrote short stories. As soon as she regained a little of her strength, she began touring across the states again. Interested as ever in anything new, she had a meeting with the magician Harry Houdini and asked him wistfully if he could restore her leg. In late autumn of 1918, she decided to return to France, despite warnings of German U-boats in the North Atlantic. The ship had to zigzag its way to avoid danger, but finally Bernhardt arrived in France to the happy news that the armistice had been signed and the long, bloody war was over.

With incredible courage and will, Sarah Bernhardt continued to fight her own war against illness and old age. Although she had scaled down her spending a little, she still needed to work to support her lifestyle, her staff, and Maurice and his family. Toward the end of her life, she amused herself by sitting down with Lysiane's husband, Louis Verneuil, and calculating her lifetime earnings. She estimated that she had made a total of more that 45 million gold francs, or $9 million, plus 450 million paper francs. Yet, she had no savings. After her operation, she lived on loans, by selling her jewelry, and by what she could make from her acting.

Louis Verneuil wrote a four-act play called *Daniel* for Bernhardt, which lent itself to her limited mobility. After a successful opening in Paris, she took it on a European tour, although she and critics knew it was a poor piece of work for a great actress to appear in. Her audiences knew it, too, but they came and applauded and cheered out of love and loyalty. They also suspected that it was probably the last time they would see the great Sarah Bernhardt.

She continued to appear in other plays adapted to her disability, and in 1921 had her last season on the London stage. While there she gave a royal command performance and had a pleasant visit with her friend Queen Mary. Back in Paris, she bravely continued her professional and social life. The famous French author Colette, who was invited to tea, left a touching picture of the visit:

> The delicate and withered hand offering the brimming cup, the flowery azure of the eyes, so young still in their network of fine lines, the questioning and mocking coquetry of the tilted head, and that indestructible desire to charm, to charm still, to charm right up to the gates of death itself. (Skinner, 331)

Bernhardt also continued to respond to appeals to help worthy causes, and appeared at a benefit for Madame Curie's Institute of Radium in the fall of 1922.

She was rehearsing for yet another opening of a new play when she suffered another attack of uremia in December and collapsed. When she regained consciousness, her first words were: "When do I go on?" (Skinner, 331) She had appeared for the last time on the stage, however, and was forced to take to her bed. Even then she continued to work. As soon as she gained enough strength to sit, she began work on a movie. The Hollywood company brought lights and cameras to film in her bedroom. She was pleased that they were paying her 10,000 francs a day, and she talked about her next American tour.

On March 21, she lapsed into a state of semi-consciousness, and she died five days later in Maurice's arms. She was laid in her famous coffin, dressed in white satin, with her head resting on a pillow of violets surrounded by roses and lilacs, a silver cross in her hand, the ribbon of the Legion of Honour on her

Bernhardt's funeral cortege, Paris, April 6, 1923. Thirty thousand people filed by the body of "The Bernhardt" as it lay in state. Grieving fans filled the streets of Paris as her vast funeral cortege—shown here outside the church of St. Augustine—progressed from the Church of St. François de Sales to the famous Père Lachaise Cemetery, stopping for a respectful moment outside the Sarah Bernhardt Theatre. Mountains of flowers marked the mourners' adulation, and, by Bernhardt's request, schoolchildren walked beside the coffin. Also at Bernhardt's request, and despite the legions of distinguished artistic and political figures in attendance, no speeches were made at her gravesite.

breast, and the gold locket containing Maurice's picture and a lock of his hair around her neck.

Thousands of people lined the streets to watch her funeral procession. When the cortege stopped for a few moments in front of the Sarah Bernhardt Theatre, showers of multicolored flowers floated down from the roof to cover the coffin below. She was buried in the Père Lachaise Cemetery beneath a tombstone marked only with her surname. At her request, there were no speeches at her gravesite, but one young actress, overwhelmed by the death of her idol, could not help crying out, "Immortals do not die!" It was an epitaph Sarah Bernhardt would have appreciated.

1844   Born on October 23 in Paris.

1860   Enters the Conservatoire.

1862–63   Debuts at the Comédie Française.

1863–64   Debuts at the Gymnase.

1864   Birth of her son, Maurice, on December 22.

1866   Odéon engagement.

1870–71   Franco-Prussian War; Bernhardt organizes a hospital at the Odéon.

1872   Leaves the Odéon and rejoins the Française.

1874   Death of sister Régina.

1876   Death of mother.

1879   Premieres in London; begins business relationship with Edward Jarrett.

1880   Resigns from the Française; forms her own company; first American tour.

1881   Grand tour of Europe.

1882   Marries Damala on April 4; takes over the Ambigu Theatre.

1883   Legal separation from Damala; takes over the Porte Saint-Martin Theater.

1886   Tour of North and South America; death of Jarrett.

1887   Moves to Boulevard Pereire; Maurice marries Terka Jablonowska.

1888   Twelve-month European tour.

1889	Death of Damala.
1891	World tour, lasting until 1893.
1893	Takes over Renaissance Theatre until 1899.
1896	Brief American tour.
1899	Takes over Nations Theatre, which is renamed the Sarah Bernhardt Theatre (Théâtre Sarah-Bernhardt).
1900	American tour.
1902	European tour.
1905	American tour.
1908	Last grand tour of Europe.
1910	American tour.
1912	American tour.
1913	Receives the Legion of Honour.
1915	Amputation of leg; entertains World War I troops in France.
1916	Final "Farewell Tour" of America, lasting until 1918.
1921	Last season on the London stage.
1923	Sarah Bernhardt dies at home in Paris on March 26.

Works by Sarah Bernhardt

Books

Dans les Nuages: Impressions d'une Chaise Charpentier, 1878
(*In the Clouds*: Bernhardt's whimsical account of the *Doña Sol*
expedition with Clairin)

L'Aveu, 1888

Adrienne Lecouvreur, 1907

Ma Double Vie, 1907 (published in English as *My Double Life,* 1908)

Un Coeur d'Homme, 1911

Petite Idole Roman, 1920

The Idol of Paris Cecil Palmer, 1921

L'Art du Théâtre, 1923 (published in English as *The Art of the
Theatre,* 1924)

Principal Performances

Le Passant, 1869: Bernhardt's first success with critics and public.

Ruy Blas, 1872: Great success as the unhappy queen of Spain.

Phèdre, 1874: Classic role revealed her acting genius.

Hernani, 1877: Literary and political revival of Hugo's play; origin of
nickname Doña Sol.

La Dame aux Camélias, 1880: The most popular of all her roles.

Fédora, 1882: Bernhardt originated the title role.

Théodora, 1884: Bernhardt originated the title role.

La Tosca, 1887: Bernhardt created the role of Floria Tosca.

Jeanne d'Arc, 1890: At age 45, played the 19-year-old French martyr.

Cléopâtre, 1890: Bernhardt created the principal role in this play
by Sardou.

Hamlet, 1899: Bernhardt portrayed Hamlet, a role usually reserved
for men.

L'Aiglon, 1900: Bernhardt played Napoleon's pathetic son, the
Duc de Reichstadt.

Francesca da Rimini, 1902: Bernhardt premiered in London in the
title role.

Adrienne Lecouvreur, 1905: Starred in her own version of play.

Le Procès de Jeanne d'Arc [*The Trial of Joan of Arc*], 1909: Bernhart played, at the age of 65, the 19-year-old Joan.

Lucrèce Borgia, 1911: Bernhardt performed the title role in Victor Hugo's play.

La Reine Elisabeth [*Queen Elizabeth*], 1912: Bernhardt played Elizabeth I of England.

La Mort de Cléopâtre, 1913: Bernhardt premiered this one-act play in London.

Athalie, 1920: Bernhardt opened in Paris in title role.

Daniel, 1921: Bernhardt created the title role in this play by her grandson-in-law.

Régine Armand, 1922: Her final role.

Bibliography

Aston, Elaine. *Sarah Bernhardt: A French Actress on the English Stage.* Berg, 1989.

Bernhardt, Lysiane S. *Sarah Bernhardt, Ma Grand'Mère.* Éditions du Pavis, 1945 (published in English as *Sarah Bernhardt, My Grandmother.* Hurst & Blackett, 1949).

Bernhardt, Sarah. *The Art of the Theatre* [*L'Art du Théâtre*], trans. H.J. Stenning. Bles, 1924.

———. *My Double Life* [*Ma Double Vie*], trans. Victoria Tietze Larson. State University of New York Press, 1999.

Carey, Gary. *Marlon Brando: The Only Contender.* St. Martin's Press, 1985.

Gold, Arthur, and Robert Fizdale. *The Divine Sarah: A Life of Sarah Bernhardt.* Alfred A. Knopf, 1991.

Richardson, Joanna. *Sarah Bernhardt and Her World.* G. Putnam's Sons, 1977.

Skinner, Cornelia Otis. *Madame Sarah.* Houghton Mifflin, 1967.

Arthur, Sir George. *Sarah Bernhardt.* William Heinemann, 1923.

Aston, Elaine. *Sarah Bernhardt: A French Actress on the English Stage.* Berg, 1989.

Baring, Maurice. *Sarah Bernhardt.* Peter Davies, 1933.

Bernhardt, Sarah. *The Art of the Theatre [L'Art du Théâtre],* trans. H.J. Stenning. Bles, 1924.

———. *In the Clouds,* in *The Memoirs of Sarah Bernhardt.* Peebles Press, 1977.

———. *The Memoirs of Sarah Bernhardt,* ed. Sandy Lesberg. Peebles Press, 1977.

———. "Men's Roles as Played by Women." *Harper's Bazaar* 33 (December 15, 1900):2113.

Brandon, Ruth. *Being Divine: A Biography of Sarah Bernhardt.* Martin Secker & Warburg Limited, 1991.

Colombier, Marie. *Le Voyage de Sarah Bernhardt en Amérique.* M. Dreyfous, 1882.

De Polnay, Peter. *Sarah Bernhardt.* Heron Books, 1970.

Fraser, Corille. *Come to Dazzle: Sarah Bernhardt's Australian Tour.* Currency Press, 1998.

Gallus, A. *Sarah Bernhardt: Her Artistic Life.* R.H. Russell, 1901.

Gold, Arthur, and Robert Fizdale. *The Divine Sarah: A Life of Sarah Bernhardt.* Alfred A. Knopf, 1991.

Hathorn, Ramon. *Our Lady of the Snows: Sarah Bernhardt in Canada.* Peter Lang, 1996.

Huret, Jules. *Sarah Bernhardt.* Chapman & Hall, 1899.

Izard, Forrest. *Sarah Bernhardt: An Appreciation.* Strugis & Walton, 1915.

Knepler, Henry. *Gilded Stage: The Lives & Careers of Four Great Actresses: Rachel Felix, Adelaide Ristori, Sarah Bernhardt, & Eleonora Duse.* Constable, 1968.

Richardson, Joanna. *Sarah Bernhardt and Her World.* G. Putnam's Sons, 1977.

Row, William Arthur. *Sarah the Divine Comet.* Press, 1957.

Rueff, Suze. *I Knew Sarah Bernhardt.* Muller, 1951.

Further Reading

Sagan, Françoise. *Dear Sarah Bernhardt.* Macmillan, 1989.

Salmon, Eric, ed. *Bernhardt and the Theatre of Her Time.* Greenwood, 1984.

Skinner, Cornelia Otis. *Madame Sarah.* Houghton Mifflin, 1967.

Stokes, John, Michael R. Booth, and Susan Bassnett. *Bernhardt, Berry, Duse: The Actress in Her Time.* Cambridge University Press, 1988.

Taranow, Gerda. *Sarah Bernhardt: The Art Within the Legend.* Princeton University Press, 1972.

Verneuil, Louis. *The Fabulous Life of Sarah Bernhardt* [*La Vie Merveilleuse de Sarah Bernhardt*], trans. Ernest Boyd. Harper & Brothers, 1942.

Wagenknecht, Edward. *Seven Daughters of the Theater: Jenny Lind, Sarah Bernhardt, Ellen Terry, Julia Marlowe, Isadora Duncan, Mary Garden, Marilyn Monroe.* University of Oklahoma Press, 1964.

Wilde, Oscar. *Oscar Wilde's Letters to Sarah Bernhardt.* Haldeman-Julius Company, 1900.

Woon, Basil. *The Real Sarah Bernhardt.* Boni and Liveright, 1924.

Websites

The Sarah Bernhardt Pages
www.sarah-bernhardt.com

Plays, books, photographs
www.users.globalnet.co.uk/~temple/sarah.htm

Photographs of Sarah Bernhardt
silent-movies.com/Ladies/OSL Bernhardt.html

Studio Postcards of Sarah Bernhardt
shakespeare.cc.emory.edu

Théâtre Sarah-Bernhardt
www.paris.org

and rescuing family from
Hamburg, Germany, 52-53
and retreat on Belle Île, 19,
104-108, 111
and Sarah Bernhardt Theatre,
108-110, 111, 119
and Scandinavian tour, 92
and school play, 30, 34
and sedan chair, 114
and short stories, 116
son of. *See* Bernhardt, Maurice
and South American tours,
94-96, 111
and stage debut as child, 34
and stage fright, 19, 30, 42, 59, 68-70
as teenager, 34-37
and temper fits, 30, 31, 32, 34,
41, 42, 43-45
uremia, 116, 117
and voice, 14, 40, 41, 54
wealth of, 41-42, 76-77, 84, 96,
103, 110, 116, 117
and whale publicity, 81-82
and world tour, 20, 103
and World War I, 20, 113-114, 116
Bernhardt, Simone (granddaughter),
100
"Bernhardt Special" (private train),
15, 77-78
Boarding school, Bernhardt attending, 28-31
Boston, Bernhardt's shows in, 17,
81-82
Boulevard Pierre, Bernhardt's home
on, 96, 111
Brabender, Mademoiselle, 35
Brazil, Bernhardt's shows in, 94
Brittany
Bernhardt living with wet nurse
in, 26-27
Bernhardt's retreat on, 19, 104-
108, 111

Brussels, Bernhardt's shows in, 75
Buenos Aires, Bernhardt's shows
in, 95

Camille (play), 110
Canada, Bernhardt's shows in, 17,
82-84, 84
Caroline, Miss, 30
Chester Square, Bernhard's home
in London in, 67, 71
Chicago, Bernhardt's shows in, 17,
84
Chile, Bernhardt's shows in, 95
Cincinnati, Bernhardt's shows in,
84
Clairin, Georges, 56, 58, 62-63, 71,
108
Clemenceau, Georges, 114
Cleopatra (play), 101, 103
Clergy, Bernhardt criticized by, 15,
17, 82-83
Coffin
Bernhardt buried in, 117, 119
Bernhardt sleeping in, 57
as gift from Bernhardt's mother,
36, 57
Colette, 117
Colombier, Marie, 50, 79, 85
Comédie Française
and asking Bernhardt to return
to, 75
Bernhardt acting at, 55, 56, 59,
61
Bernhardt as *pensionnaire* at,
41-45
and Bernhardt's animals in
London, 71-73
Bernhardt's break with, 71-74
Bernhardt's debut at, 20, 41-42
Bernhardt's departure from, 45
Bernhardt seeing first real play
in, 37

Index

Bernhardt settling suit with, 74
and Bernhardt's hot-air balloon
ride, 61-63
Bernhardt's return to, 55-56
and Bernhardt's sculpting
costume, 58
Bernhardt's temper fit in, 43-45
at London's Gaiety Theatre, 63,
66, 68-70
Commune, 53-54
Conservatoire (Conservatory of
Music and Drama), Bernhardt
attending, 36, 38-41
Convent school, Bernhardt attend-
ing, 30-31, 34-35
Cooper, James Fenimore, 78
Copenhagen, Bernhardt's shows
in, 75
Coppée, François, 49
Courtesan
Bernhardt's aunt as, 27
Bernhardt's mother as, 25-26
Covent Garden, 74
Croizette, Sophie, 55-56
Cross, Mr., 71
Cross Zoo (Liverpool), 70-71
Curie, Madame, 117

Damala, Aristidis ("Jacques")
(husband), 85, 87, 89, 90, 92-93,
100
*Dame aux Camélias, La (The Lady
of the Camellias)*
film, 112
play, 17, 20, 61, 78, 81, 84, 87,
92, 98, 109
Daniel (play), 116-117
Darwin (monkey), 70, 71
Detroit, Bernhardt's shows in,
84
Dom Pedro II, emperor of Brazil,
94

Doña Sol (airship), 62-63
Doña Sol, as affectionate name for
Bernhardt, 61
Doré, Gustave, 58, 71
Dumas *fils*, Alexandre, 40, 78
Dumas *père*, Alexandre, 38, 39-40,
47
Duquesnel, Felix, 46

Ecuador, Bernhardt's shows in, 95
Egypt, Bernhardt's shows in, 100
England. *See* London
European tours
1881–1882, 85, 87, 89
1886, 95-96
1888, 100
1908–1909, 110
1919, 116-117

"Farewell American Tours," 110,
114, 116
Faure, Henriette (aunt), 29, 30, 31,
32, 35
Faure, Uncle, 29-30, 31
Fédora (play), 89, 92
Filmmaking, Bernhardt involved
in, 117
Fishing, at Belle Île, 107
France, Anatole, 101, 103
Franco-Prussian War, 49-51
French Fête, 70
French Hospital (London), 70
Fressard, Madame, 28-31, 31
Froufrou (play), 75, 78, 92

Gaiety Theatre
Bernhardt's contract with, 74-75
Comédie Française at, 33, 66,
68-70
Gauthier, Marguérite, 17
Giffard, Henri, 61-62
Gladstone, William, 70

130

Index

Index

Credits

Contributors

Elizabeth Silverthorne is a freelance writer who lives in the village of Salado, Texas. She has B.A. and M.A. degrees from North Texas State University in Denton, Texas, and has studied writing at the University of Texas, The Institute in San Miguel de Allende, Mexico, and the Bread Loaf Writer's School. She is a Fellow of the Texas State Historical Society. She taught English and Children's Literature at North Texas State University for four years and was Director of Communications and Modern Languages at Temple College for 12 years. Her works include numerous articles and short stories for children and adults, as well as 17 books. She has written biographies of Ashbel Smith of Texas, Sarah Orne Jewett, and Marjorie Kinnan Rawlings. For Chelsea House, she has written biographies of Louisa May Alcott and Anton Chekhov.

Congresswoman Betty McCollum (Minnesota, Fourth District) is the second woman from Minnesota ever to have been elected to Congress. Since the start of her first term of office in 2000, she has worked diligently to protect the environment and to expand access to health care, and she has been an especially strong supporter of education and women's health care. She holds several prominent positions in the House Democratic Caucus and enjoys the rare distinction of serving on three House Committees at once. In 2001, she was appointed to represent the House Democrats on the National Council on the Arts, the advisory board of the National Endowment for the Arts.